Andrew Edney

POWERPOINT 2007

In easy steps is an imprint of Computer Step
Southfield Road · Southam
Warwickshire CV47 0FB · United Kingdom
www.ineasysteps.com

Notice of Liability
Every effort has been made to ensure that this book contains accurate
and current information. However, Computer Step and the author
shall not be liable for any loss or damage suffered by readers as a
result of any information contained herein.

Trademarks
Microsoft® and Windows® are registered trademarks of Microsoft
Corporation. All other trademarks are acknowledged as belonging to
their respective companies.

Printed and bound in the United Kingdom

ISBN-13 978-1-84078-327-8
ISBN-10 1-84078-327-3

Contents

12 Security   175

Index   187

1 PowerPoint 2007

This chapter will introduce you to some of the new features of PowerPoint 2007 and will begin to show you some of the different ways of doing things, including how to diagnose and fix problems with PowerPoint and Office and how to update PowerPoint 2007.

What is PowerPoint?

You probably already know that PowerPoint is a software package designed to help you create professional looking presentations as easily as possible, and it has been around for a number of years.

The latest incarnation, PowerPoint 2007, continues the tradition of providing you with all the tools you need to create and distribute your presentations, and goes that little bit further by including a number of new and exciting features that make your presentations look even more professional and of a higher quality than they did before.

PowerPoint 2007 enables you to:

- Create professional looking presentations
- Share presentations with anyone from colleagues to customers
- Add sounds, video, pictures and more to presentations
- Create standalone presentations for use in kiosks and on booths at trade shows
- Allows others to review and comment on your presentations and even use workflow processes
- Secure your presentations using Information Rights Management technologies
- And much, much more

Microsoft Office 2007 Versions

There are five different versions of Microsoft Office 2007 that are currently available:

- Office Home and Student
- Office Standard
- Office Small Business
- Office Professional
- Office Ultimate

Each one of the five Microsoft Office 2007 versions contains PowerPoint 2007, so it doesn't matter which version you buy, you will still get access to PowerPoint.

Hot tip

If you already have Office 2003 installed on your computer, you can purchase an Upgrade version which is less expensive than the full version.

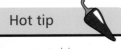

Hot tip

You can test drive Microsoft Office from your Internet browser by going to http://www.microsoft.com/office.

Hot tip

Check out what comes with each version of Microsoft Office 2007 and make sure you purchase the version that is right for you.

PowerPoint Requirements

In order to be able to install and use PowerPoint 2007, you will need to ensure that your computer meets the minimum requirements for running PowerPoint 2007, which are as follows:

Component	Requirement
Processor	500 MHz Processor or higher
Memory	256 MB RAM or higher
Hard Disk	1 GB free
Drive	CD-ROM or DVD Drive
Display	1024 x 768 or higher resolution monitor
Operating System	Minimum Windows XP with SP2, Windows Server 2003 with SP1, Windows Vista
Other	Certain Inking features require Windows XP Tablet PC Edition or later; Speech recognition functionality requires a close-talk microphone and audio output device; Information Rights Management features requires Windows 2003 Server with SP1 or later running Windows Rights Management Service; Internet Explorer 6.0 or later; Collaboration requires Windows SharePoint Services; PowerPoint Slide Libraries require Office SharePoint Server 2007
Additional	Actual requirements and product functionality may vary based on system configuration and operating system

9

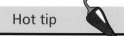

Hot tip

If you are planning on installing and running PowerPoint 2007, on any version of Windows Vista, you should consider increasing the processor and memory compared to that listed in the minimum requirements.

Beware

If you are planning on using Windows Vista as your operating system, you should ensure your computer is capable of running the version of Vista you want to use.

New and Improved Features

PowerPoint 2007 introduces a wealth of new and improved features that are designed to help you to create professional looking presentations and get the most out of the product without you having to do every little thing yourself.

Some of these new and improved features include:

- A new intuitive user interface called the Ribbon

- Improved effects, themes and enhanced formatting options

- The ability to use a Live preview that shows you the result of what you can select without having to actually select it

- A number of predefined Quick Styles that include layouts, tables formats, effects and more

- The ability to initiate workflow processes

- SmartArt graphics that can be used to quickly and easily produce high quality designer-style graphics

- The new XML file format which reduces the size of the file and also provides enhanced recovery abilities

- Enhancements and improvements for tables and charts

- A new Presenter View which enables you to run your presentation on one monitor while you view something different on another monitor, which can make the task of actually delivering your presentation that much easier

- Slide Libraries which enable you to share and reuse content from your slides. Slide Libraries require Microsoft Office SharePoint Server 2007

- The ability to save your presentations as a PDF

- A number of security-related functions, including enhanced Information Rights Management, and the ability to find and remove hidden metadata from your presentations. You can also add digital signatures to your presentations

- Office Diagnostics to help diagnose, troubleshoot and repair problems you might experience with any of your Microsoft Office 2007 applications

Beware

Some of the new features require additional software, such as Microsoft Office SharePoint Server 2007, in order to make them work and may also require additional hardware.

10

Installing PowerPoint 2007

If you have not yet installed PowerPoint 2007 then now is the time to do so.

1 Insert the Microsoft Office 2007 CD into your computer

2 If the setup program does not start automatically, double-click on setup.exe on the CD to start it

3 Enter your 25-character Product Key then click Continue

4 Click Install Now to perform a standard installation or click Customize to select what you want to install

Hot tip

You can check out all of the new features of PowerPoint 2007, and other Office 2007 applications, by downloading a trial version from http://www.microsoft.com/office.

Don't forget

You will need a valid Product Key to install Microsoft Office 2007.

...cont'd

Hot tip

If you want to install all of the available programs, just select Run all from My Computer when clicking on Microsoft Office.

Don't forget

Make sure you have enough available free disk space in order to install all of the Microsoft Office programs that you have selected.

5 If you clicked on Customize, work through the available programs and select whether or not to install each one

> Installation Options | File Location | User Information
>
> Customize how Microsoft Office programs run
>
> Microsoft Office
> - Microsoft Office Access
> - Microsoft Office Excel
> - Microsoft Office Groove
> - Microsoft Office InfoPath
> - Microsoft Office OneNote
> - Microsoft Office Outlook
> - Microsoft Office PowerPoint
> - Microsoft Office Publisher
> - Microsoft Office Visio Viewer
> - Microsoft Office Word
> - Office Shared Features
> - Office Tools
>
> Microsoft Office productivity programs plus additional content and tools.
>
> Total space required on drive: 1775 MB
> Space available on drive: 225235 MB
>
> Install Now

6 Click on the File Location tab to select where on your computer to install the chosen Office 2007 programs

7 Click on the User Information tab and enter your details in the Full Name, Initials and Organization boxes, then click the Install Now button

> Installation Options | File Location | User Information
>
> **Type your information**
>
> Type your full name, initials, and organization.
>
> This information is used by Microsoft Office programs to identify the person who makes changes in a shared Office document.
>
> Full Name: Andrew Edney
>
> Initials: AE
>
> Organization: Firebird Consulting

Starting PowerPoint 2007

Before you can start to create your presentations, you have to start PowerPoint 2007. There are different ways you can do this.

The Start Menu
Like any application, you can start PowerPoint by selecting it from the Start Menu.

1 Click on the Start button

2 Click on All Programs

3 Click on Microsoft Office

4 Double-click on Microsoft Office PowerPoint 2007

Hot tip
You can also add PowerPoint 2007 to the Quick Launch area on your desktop by dragging it there.

13

Creating a Shortcut
You can create a shortcut icon on your desktop to enable you to quickly launch PowerPoint.

1 From the Start Menu, click and hold the Microsoft Office PowerPoint 2007 icon

2 Drag the mouse to the desktop and release the button to create the shortcut

Don't forget
You can also start PowerPoint 2007 by double-clicking on any PowerPoint presentation that you have access to.

Creating a New Presentation
You can create a new presentation and then launch it.

1 Click the right mouse button and click New, followed by Microsoft Office PowerPoint Presentation

2 Name the new file, then double-click it to launch it and start creating your slides

Exploring the Ribbon

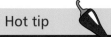
The Ribbon is the replacement for the various menus and toolbars that you may be used to if you have used a previous version of PowerPoint. Apart from looking completely different, the Ribbon provides both contextual tabs and menus. What this means is that different options will be available to you depending on what you are doing and what you select. This reduces the clutter of menus and toolbars that you may not need very often, and provides you with the menus you need to use when you need to use them.

Tabs

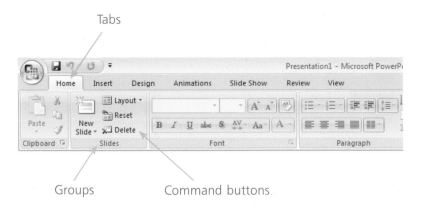

Groups   Command buttons

The various commands are grouped together logically under different tabs. Each of the tabs relates to a different activity and includes various command buttons. The initial tabs that are available to use are:

- Home – includes command groups and buttons for the clipboard, slides, fonts, paragraphs, drawing and editing

- Insert – includes command groups and buttons for tables, illustrations, links, text and media clips

- Design – includes command groups and buttons for page setup, themes and backgrounds

- Animations – includes command groups and buttons for previewing, animations and transitions

- Slide Show – includes command groups and buttons for starting slide shows, setting up slide shows and monitor settings

● Review – includes command groups and buttons for proofing, comments and protecting your presentation

● View – includes command groups and buttons for presentation views, show/hide functions, zoom, color/grayscale use, windows and using macros

There are two additional kinds of tabs that can appear when they are needed – Contextual tabs and Program tabs.

Contextual Tabs

Contextual tabs appear when you select an object, such as a picture or text box. Depending on what you select, a contextual tab will appear. For example, if you select a text box, the Drawing Tools tab will appear.

Contextual tab

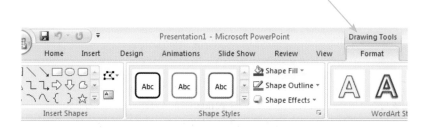

Program Tabs

Program tabs appear when certain modes or views are used, such as Print Preview, and they replace the standard tabs for the duration of the action.

Program tab

Hot tip

If you need to hide the Ribbon at any time just press CTRL + F1 to hide it and then press CTRL + F1 again to restore it.

15

2003 Commands in 2007

If you are familiar with using PowerPoint 2003, then you will probably notice that PowerPoint 2007 looks completely different. A major difference is that some of the commands you might be comfortable using are either no longer there or are not obvious as to their location.

There are a few different ways to familiarize yourself with the 2007 commands. One very useful tool, that Microsoft provide, is an Interactive PowerPoint 2003 to PowerPoint 2007 command reference guide that uses Macromedia Flash in order to show you the new location of commands by clicking on a PowerPoint 2003 environment.

Hot tip

You will need to have the Macromedia Flash Player installed in order to use the Interactive reference guide. If you don't have it installed you will be prompted to install it the first time you click on Start the guide.

1. From your Internet browser, go to: http://office. microsoft.com/en-us/powerpoint/HA101490761033. aspx?pid=CD100668131033

2. Click Start the guide

3. When the guide begins click the Start button

4. Highlight the PowerPoint 2003 command you are used to using to see the new location in PowerPoint 2007

5. If you click on the PowerPoint 2003 command, you will be treated to a brief demo of where the PowerPoint 2007 command is located

6. Click the Close Window button to end the session

Hot tip

There is also a Ribbon Mapping Workbook which can be downloaded from http:// office.microsoft.com/ search/redir.aspx?AssetID =AM101923921033&CT T=5&Origin=HA100666 231033 and contains all the old commands and their new locations. Keep it handy until you are completely comfortable with the location of all of your favorite commands.

The Microsoft Office Button

If you are familiar with previous versions of PowerPoint, or other Microsoft Office applications, you will have used the File menu at some point to save, print or perform any number of possible tasks.

PowerPoint 2007 does not have a File menu, instead it uses something called The Microsoft Office Button. This appears in the upper-left corner on all Microsoft Office 2007 applications.

1 To launch the menu just click on the Microsoft Office Button

Microsoft Office Button

Hot tip

You can shut down PowerPoint from this menu by clicking on the Exit PowerPoint button.

2 Click on whichever menu item you want to use or that you want to expand

3 Click on the item in the box that you want to use, for example, Print Preview

Quick Access Toolbar

The Quick Access Toolbar is a toolbar that is completely customizable by you to include any commands that you might use on a regular basis, such as Save or Print. Rather than work your way through the menus, you can just click the relevant command on the Quick Access Toolbar to activate the command.

Quick Access Toolbar

Customizing the Quick Access Toolbar

You can add or remove commands from the Quick Access Toolbar whenever you need to. There are a few different ways of adding commands.

1 Highlight the command you want to add to the Quick Access Toolbar

2 Click on the right mouse button and select Add to Quick Access Toolbar from the menu

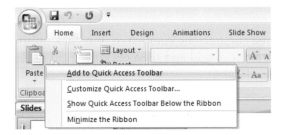

Another way involves you selecting from a list of the commands within PowerPoint 2007, and then choosing whichever one you want to add to the Quick Access Toolbar from the Customize menu of PowerPoint Options.

1 Click on the Microsoft Office Button and select the PowerPoint Options button

2 Click on Customize

Hot tip

You can also launch the Customize menu by selecting Customize Quick Access Toolbar when you right-click on any command.

[PowerPoint Options dialog box showing the Customize the Quick Access Toolbar settings, with categories Popular, Proofing, Save, Advanced, Customize, Add-Ins, Trust Center, Resources on the left. "Choose commands from: Popular Commands" list on the left with commands including Separator, Action, Bring Forward, Bring to Front, Custom Animation..., Draw Table, Draw Vertical Text Box, Duplicate Selected Slides, E-mail, Format Background..., Format Shape, Group, Insert Hyperlink, Insert Picture from File, Layout, New, New Slide, Open, Paste Special..., Print Preview, Quick Print, Redo, Regroup, Reuse Slides... and "Customize Quick Access Toolbar: For all documents (default)" showing Save, Undo, Redo. Add >> and Remove buttons in the middle. Reset and Modify... buttons at the bottom, with "Show Quick Access Toolbar below the Ribbon" checkbox, and OK / Cancel buttons.]

Hot tip

You can customize the Quick Access Toolbar for all of your PowerPoint 2007 presentations (which is the default setting) or you can choose to only customize the toolbar for the current presentation.

19

3 Click on the Choose commands from the drop-down list then select which area you want to display the commands for

4 Scroll through the commands and click on the command you want to add and then click the Add button

5 Repeat steps 3 through 5 until you have added all of the commands you want to the Toolbar

6 Use the up and down arrows to reorder the commands in the Quick Access Toolbar list until you are happy, and then click the OK button to finish customizing the Quick Access Toolbar

Hot tip

Don't worry if you make a mistake as you can just click on the Reset button to restore the Quick Access Toolbar to its default setting.

Help and How-to

If you experience a problem or would like some help on how to do something particular with PowerPoint 2007, then help is literally at hand. PowerPoint has a detailed help and how-to component, and when you are connected to the Internet this is expanded to include additional content and anything else new.

Hot tip

You can also launch the Help and How-to dialog box by pressing F1 on your keyboard.

1 Click on the Help button on the Ribbon (its the ?) near the top right-hand corner of the screen

2 Click on any entry to see additional topics

Hot tip

Ensure your computer is connected to the Internet in order to search online for more up to date content.

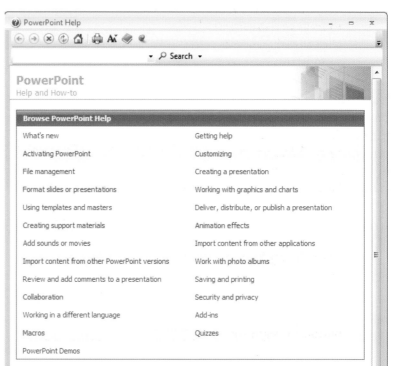

3 Click on one of the newly displayed topics to see the help or how-to information for that particular topic

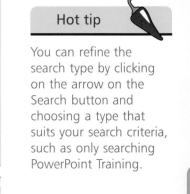

Hot tip

You can refine the search type by clicking on the arrow on the Search button and choosing a type that suits your search criteria, such as only searching PowerPoint Training.

4 Click the Print icon if you want to print it

5 Click the Back icon to return to the list or click the Home icon to return to the start

Manual Searching

You can also enter text into the search box to look for something specific instead of trying to find it from the various lists.

1 Enter a word, phrase or text entry into the search box

2 Click the Search button to begin the search

Beware

If you are searching Office Online, you will also see results for other Office applications and different versions of PowerPoint (unless you consider refining your search).

Search Locations

You can choose to search for content from Office Online or only from the local computer.

1 Click the Connection Status box and select the location

21

Fixing PowerPoint & Office

From time to time things can and do go wrong with both PowerPoint and also with other Office programs installed on your computer. Fortunately Microsoft have provided the Microsoft Office Diagnostics tool which is used to diagnose and repair a number of problems that can occur. These diagnostics include:

- Checking for known solutions to problems you have recently experienced if PowerPoint or Office had crashed

- Performing memory diagnostics against your installed RAM

- Performing compatibility diagnostics against installations

- Performing disk diagnostics against your hard drives

- Performing setup diagnostics against files and the registry

1   Click on the Office button and select PowerPoint options

2   Click on Resources and then click Diagnose to run Microsoft Office Diagnostics

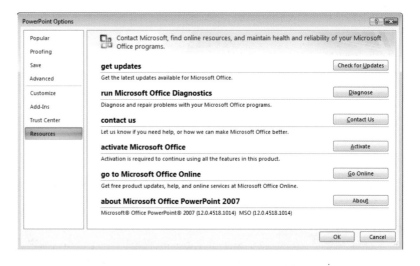

3   Click on Continue

4   Click Run Diagnostics to start

Microsoft Office Diagnostics

Start Diagnostics

		Status:	
	Check for known solutions	**Status:**	Ready to run
	Memory Diagnostic	**Status:**	Ready to run
	Compatibility Diagnostic	**Status:**	Ready to run
	Disk Diagnostic	**Status:**	Ready to run
	Setup Diagnostic	**Status:**	Ready to run

What will diagnostics do?   Run Diagnostics   Cancel

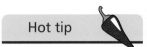
The diagnostics will now be performed and this can often take up to around 15 minutes to complete. After they have completed, you will be presented with a results screen.

Microsoft Office Diagnostics

No cause found.

The diagnostic tests found no problems. Click Continue to connect to Microsoft's servers and view recommended next steps.

Summary of results:

Diagnostics run: 5
Diagnostics that identified problems: 0
Diagnostics that took corrective actions: 0

Detailed results   Continue   Cancel

5   Click Continue to launch Internet Explorer and you will be presented with suggestions on how to fix any problems that might have been found

6   If no problems were detected just click Cancel to finish

Office Online

The Microsoft Office Online website provides a wealth of useful tools, guides, downloads and more, that are invaluable to any Microsoft Office user.

To access certain online services content you will need to register on the site.

1 Click the Microsoft Office Button and select PowerPoint Options

2 Click on Resources and then select the Go Online button from the go to Microsoft Office Online section

3 Click the Register for free online service button

4 Sign in with your Microsoft Passport Account

5 Complete the Microsoft Office Online Registration form

6 Click the Update button at the bottom of the form

You will then be taken to an area that is called My Office Online. From here you can change your registration preferences, access Subscription Services, search for online content and more.

Updating PowerPoint 2007

It is very important that you keep PowerPoint 2007, and all of your Microsoft Office applications up to date. Updates are released periodically and include bug fixes and product updates so there may be something that you need. One of the simplest ways to update Office is to have Office check for updates for you.

1 Click the Microsoft Office Button and select PowerPoint Options

2 Click on Resources and then select the Go Online button from the go to Microsoft Office Online section

3 Click on Check for updates

Check for updates
- Download free updates for enhanced security and performance

4 Click on Check for Microsoft Updates and select any updates you want (if there are any)

Check for updates

Scan for the latest stability and security updates now.

Check for Microsoft Updates

Office Update: Get additional Office updates

Using Microsoft Update

The simplest and easiest way by far is to install Microsoft Update and allow it to manage all of your updates, including Microsoft Office and Windows Vista. To use Microsoft Update just click on Windows Update in Vista and follow any prompts.

25

Windows Update with Windows Ultimate Extras

Windows is up to date

Available: 16 optional updates — View available updates
No new important updates are available for your computer.

There are Windows Ultimate Extras available for download

Extras Available: 1 — View available Extras
Hold Em Poker Game

Most recent check for updates: Today at 10:11
Updates were installed: Today at 10:13. View update history
You have Windows set to: Automatically install new updates every day at 03:00 (recommended)
You receive updates: For Windows and other products from Microsoft Update

KeyTips

You may not want to use the mouse to select items from the Ribbon or you might want to use some of the keyboard shortcuts that are available to speed up your work.

These keyboard shortcuts are known as KeyTips and are used to access a tab or perform a function by pressing a single key or series of keys from your keyboard.

Hot tip

You can also display the KeyTips by pressing the F10 key on your keyboard. .

1 Press and release the ALT key at anytime

2 Press the key that matches the action you want to perform, such as W for the View tab

Don't forget

The letter for a KeyTip in one menu might also be used in another menu so select carefully.

3 Press the key that matches the action you want to perform or press the ALT key again to cancel the KeyTips selection

Other Keyboard Shortcuts

Apart from the KeyTips there are numerous keyboard shortcuts that can be used within PowerPoint 2007.

For a detailed list of the shortcuts and their functions do a search for Keyboard Shortcuts for PowerPoint 2007 from the Office Help area. You should then be able to select the help document that contains the list.

2 Creating Presentations

This chapter will explain how to begin to create a new PowerPoint presentation, how to use templates and existing presentations and also start to show off some of the features.

The Workspace

The Workspace is where you will work with PowerPoint 2007, so it is important that you understand what each part is called and what it is used for.

The Slide Pane
This is where you will do all of your work in creating your presentations.

Placeholders
Placeholders are the dotted boxes and are used to add text, graphics and other items into your presentation.

28

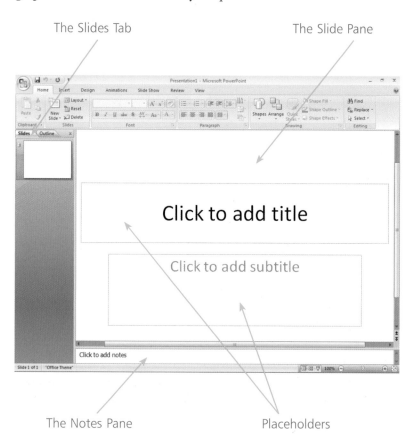

The Slides Tab   The Slide Pane

Click to add title

Click to add subtitle

The Notes Pane   Placeholders

The Slides Tab
This includes views of your slides with the current slide being highlighted.

The Notes Pane
This is where you can add notes to your presentations.

Starting a Presentation

When you first start PowerPoint 2007 you are presented with the title page to a blank presentation, which you can then use to start creating your own presentation immediately.

1 To add a title click the Click to add title placeholder and type in the title you want to use

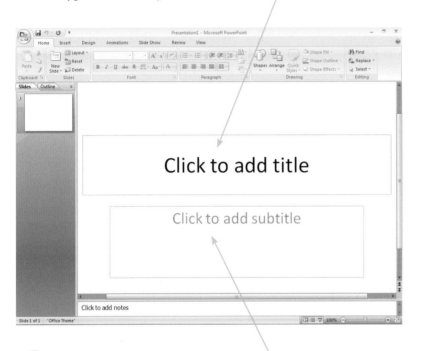

2 To add a subtitle click the Click to add subtitle placeholder and type in the text that you want to use

3 If you want to make some notes you can do so by clicking on the Click to add notes text box and typing in whatever you want to appear in the Notes view later

4 You can move around the position of the placeholders by clicking and dragging them to a new position

You can also change the background or theme, add graphics, shapes, more text and more, all of which will be covered throughout this book.

Don't forget

Whatever notes you type will not appear when you are delivering your presentation but you can include them when you print or export your presentation for others to view.

Slide Layouts

When you first start PowerPoint you will see the Title Slide layout, but there are a number of other predefined layouts that you can choose from and use in your presentations on any slide.

These predefined layouts include:

- Title and Content
- Title Only
- Blank
- Picture with Caption

You can select any of these at any time, just click in the placeholders that are provided, to easily create a slide, with the exception of the Blank layout which enables you to effectively start from scratch and create whatever look you want for the slide.

1. Ensure the Home tab is selected

2. From the Slides group click on the Layout button

3. Select the layout you want

Hot tip

If you have selected a different Theme then you will see that theme displayed along with the different layouts.

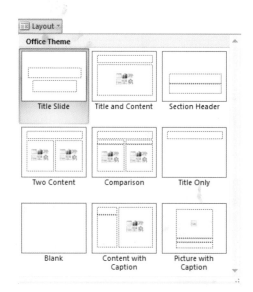

Adding Slides

You can add a new slide at any time just by clicking on the New Slide button on the Slides group.

① Ensure the Home tab is selected

② From the Slides group click on the New Slide button

③ Select the layout you want by clicking on it

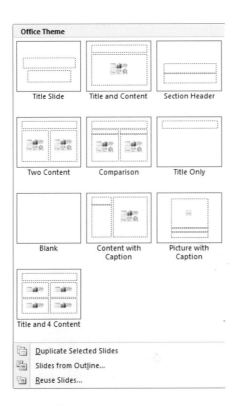

31

Duplicating Slides

You can take a complete copy of a slide, including any content that appears on it, so that you don't have to spend the time recreating a certain look or feel and then you can just amend anything on the slide itself.

Hot tip

If you want to add the same type of slide that you recently added, just click on the Slide icon rather than New Slide to repeat the previous addition.

Hot tip

You can also duplicate slides by highlighting them from the Slides view and pressing CTRL + C to copy then CTRL + P to paste.

Hot tip

You can also browse for a presentation or type in the full path to the presentation.

1 Select the slide or slides from the Slides view that you want to duplicate

2 On the Home tab, click New Slide from the Slides group

3 Click on Duplicate Selected Slides

Reusing Slides

You can now reuse slides from other presentations or from published slides in a slide library.

32

Don't forget

If you want to use a slide from a Slide Library you will need to ensure you have access to that Slide Library.

1 On the Home tab, click New Slide from the Slides group

2 Click on Reuse Slides

3 If you want to use a slide that is published in a Slide Library, click on Open a Slide Library and enter the URL of the Slide Library

4 If you want to use a slide from an existing presentation click on Open a PowerPoint File

5 Select the presentation you want to use

6 Click on the slide to add it to your presentation

Hot tip

For details on how to publish your slides to a Slide Library take a look at Chapter 11 – Sharing Presentations.

Views

There are a number of different views available to you that you might find very useful.

Normal View

Normal View is the standard PowerPoint 2007 view that appears whenever you start PowerPoint. In Normal View you can also see either the Slides View or the Outline View alongside the main presentation window.

Hot tip

The Outline view will be covered in Chapter 8 – Reviewing & Proofing.

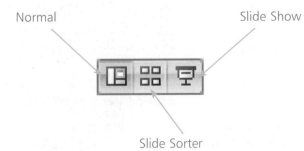

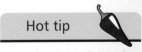

Hot tip

You can easily switch between Normal Slides view and Normal Outline view by clicking on the relevant tab.

Changing Views

The different views can be selected by clicking on the View buttons that are located at the bottom of the presentation window.

Normal   Slide Show

Slide Sorter

Hot tip

The Slide Sorter view and Slide Show view will be covered in Chapter 9 – Creating Slide Shows.

Zoom Slider

You can zoom in and out of the presentation window by using the Zoom Slider control which is located at the bottom of the presentation window.

1 Click the - or + symbols on the zoom slider to decrease or increase the presentation window size; or

2 Drag the zoom slider button to a new position

3 Click the Fit slide to current window button to fill the presentation window, if you want to do that

Before fitting slide to current window

After fitting slide to current window

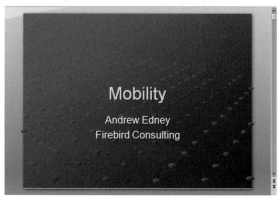

Page Layout and Orientation

The page layout and orientation you use for your slides and your presentation is very important. Depending on how you deliver your presentation, you may have a specific need to present the slides in portrait rather than the default layout which is landscape.

1   Click on the Design tab

2   Click on Page Setup

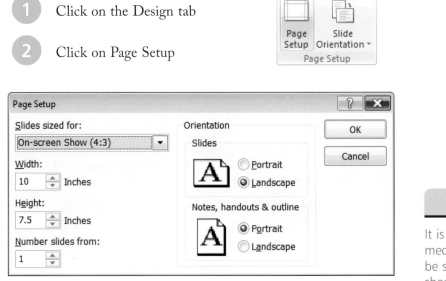

3   Select what medium the slides should be sized for from the drop-down list

4   Select the width and height in inches

5   Set the orientation for the slides and also for any notes, handouts and outlines

6   Click OK

Changing the Slide Orientation Only

1   Click on Slide Orientation

2   Select either Portrait or Landscape

Hot tip

It is worth setting what medium the slides should be sized for, as this should reduce any issues you might experience later on during your presentation delivery.

Templates and Themes

PowerPoint 2007 comes packed full of templates and themes that you can use to get your presentation started. You can then add to or change the presentation as you begin to develop it.

1 Click on the Microsoft Office Button

2 Click New from the menu

3 To start from a blank presentation or to select from recently used templates and themes, click on Blank and Recent and select the presentation you want to use

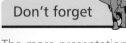
Don't forget

The more presentations you create with PowerPoint, the more selections will be available from the recently used list.

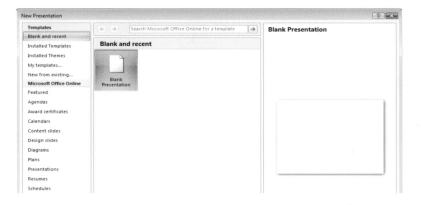

4 To select from one of the many installed Themes, click on Installed Themes and select the theme you want to use

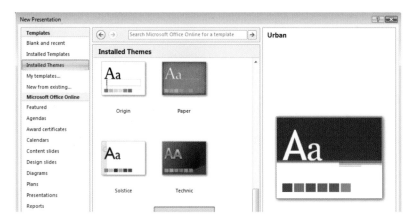

5 To select from one of the many installed Templates, click on Installed Templates and select the template you want

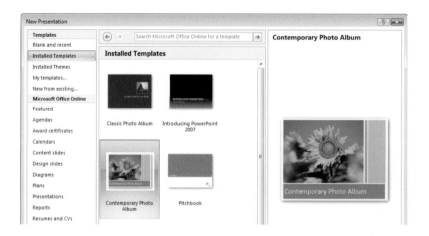

6 Click Create to create a new presentation based on your selection

7 If you have saved any templates yourself you can select them by clicking on My Templates...

8 Select the template you want to use and click OK

Hot tip

To add a template to the My Templates area you need to have saved it as a PowerPoint Template.

Downloading Presentations

You can also choose from a large amount of content that is hosted on Microsoft Office Online. To make your selection easier, this additional content is sorted into a number of different categories including:

- Diagrams and Plans

- Presentations (including some training presentations for Office 2007)

- Reports

- And much more

1   Click on the content category and select the content

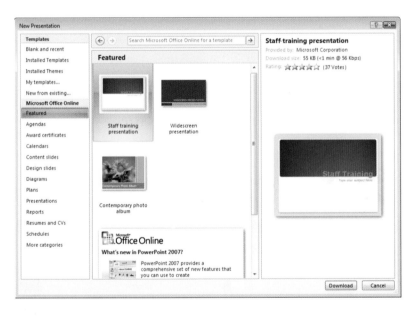

2   Click the Download button to download the content

3   You may be asked to confirm that your copy of Microsoft Office is genuine, click Continue if you are to begin the checking process

Creating Custom Layouts

If you find that none of the layouts quite suit what you require, you can always create your own custom layout, which you can then use whenever you need to. You can add many different types of placeholders to the custom layout and choose any location on the slide where you want them to appear.

 1 Click on the View tab and in the Presentations Views group select Slide Master

2 Scroll to the bottom of the slide master and layouts, then click below the last entry

3 Click on Insert Layout from the Edit Master group

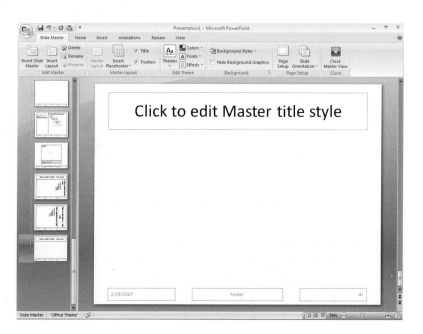

Before starting to create a new custom layout in PowerPoint, you could consider drawing it on some paper just to get an idea of what you want it to look like.

...cont'd

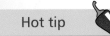

4 If you want to remove the default placeholder, click the border of the placeholder and press DEL on your keyboard

5 If you do not want footers to appear on your slide layout uncheck the Footers box from the Master Layout group

6 To start to add your placeholders, click on the Insert Placeholder button from the Master Layout group

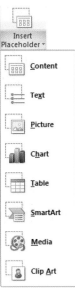

7 Select the type of Placeholder that you want to add

8 Click and hold the mouse button at the location on the layout where you want the chosen placeholder to start and then just drag it across the layout until you are happy with the size and release the button

9 Repeat steps 7 and 8 for each Placeholder that you want to add to the new layout

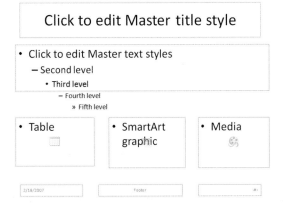

10 Save the new layout as a PowerPoint template and then click Close Master View to finish

Opening Presentations

You can open presentations from the current version of PowerPoint or from previous versions.

① Click the Microsoft Office Button

② If the presentation you want to open has been opened recently, it will appear in the Recent Documents list and you can select it from there

③ If not, click on Open

④ Search for the presentation file you want to open

⑤ Either double-click it or click it once and then click Open

41

Hot tip

If you open a presentation from a previous version of PowerPoint it is opened in Compatibility Mode – more on that on the next page.

Hot tip

If you want a presentation to always appear in the Recent Documents list, regardless of when you last opened it, you can Pin It to the list by clicking the pin icon next to the name. When the pin turns green it is pinned. Gray means it is unpinned.

Hot tip

If you click on the Open button arrow you will be presented with a number of options for opening the file, including Open as Copy and Open and Repair if the file is damaged.

Converting Presentations

If you open a presentation that was created with an earlier version of PowerPoint, it will open in what is known as Compatibility Mode. Compatibility Mode is used to suppress certain functionality within PowerPoint 2007 in order to be able to continue to work on and share the presentation with users of that earlier version of PowerPoint. Examples of the suppressed functionality can include:

Hot tip

For more information about compatibility and saving for different versions of PowerPoint see Chapter 10 – Saving Your Presentation.

- SmartArt Graphics

- Certain Quick Styles and Text Effects

You can tell you are in Compatibility Mode because [Compatibility Mode] is displayed next to the file name.

Mobility [Compatibility Mode] - Microsoft PowerPoint

You can convert the presentation to a PowerPoint 2007 format and enable all of the suppressed functionality.

Beware

Once you have converted the presentation to a PowerPoint 2007 format, you will not be able to share it with users of previous versions of PowerPoint without saving it in a previous version.

42

1 Open the presentation that was created with an earlier version of PowerPoint

2 Click on the Microsoft Office Button

New

Open

3 Select Convert from the menu

4 Click OK in the conversion dialog box

Convert

Microsoft Office PowerPoint	? X

This action will convert the document to the newest format.

Converting allows you to use all the new features of PowerPoint and reduces the size of your file. This document will be replaced by the converted version.

☐ Do not ask me again about converting documents

Tell Me More...   OK   Cancel

Hot tip

If you are going to be converting a number of presentations, it is worth checking the Do not ask me again about converting documents check box.

5 Choose a location and save the newly converted presentation file

3 Working with Text

This chapter will explain how to add and format text for use in your presentations, and how to use WordArt to make your presentations look even better.

Text

One of the main elements to your presentation is likely to be text – whether you are using text for different types of titles, lists or paragraphs of text, or a mixture of the three.

Adding Text to a New Slide

If you choose to create a new slide and select a layout that includes any sort of text box, you can just click on the text box and enter whatever text you want to appear.

1 To add a title, click on the Click to add title box placeholder and enter the text you want to use

2 To add a subtitle, click on the Click to add subtitle box placeholder and enter the text you want to use for the subtitle

Click to add title

Click to add subtitle

Adding a Text Box Placeholder to a Slide

You can also add a text box placeholder anywhere on the slide and enter any text you want into that box.

1 Click on the Insert tab and from the Text group, click on Text Box

2 Position the mouse pointer where you want to start drawing the text box, hold down the left mouse button and drag the box to the size you want then release the mouse button

3 Enter the text in the box

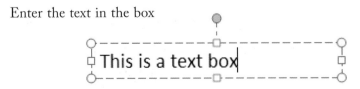

This is a text box

Hot tip

You can also copy an existing text box placeholder by selecting it and pressing CTRL + C and then CTRL + V to paste it. You can then move it to any position on the slide and edit it.

AutoFit

If you have entered more text into a text placeholder than the placeholder can actually contain, you may have noticed that the text you entered automatically resizes to a smaller font in order to fit all of the text into the placeholder. This function is called AutoFit and can be very useful to ensure that everything you want to enter into a text placeholder is actually displayed. This works by first reducing the amount of line spacing and then reducing the font size.

1 If you are entering some text and you fill up the placeholder, the Autofit Options button will appear

> The Year End Results for Fiscal Year 2007 and the plan for year 2008

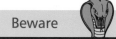

Beware

Be careful not to enter too much text otherwise it may become so small that it is unreadable.

2 If you want to AutoFit the text to the placeholder just keep typing and it will be automatically adjusted

3 If you do not want to AutoFit the text, click on the AutoFit Options button

⊙ AutoFit Text to Placeholder
○ Stop Fitting Text to This Placeholder
🌀 Control AutoCorrect Options...

4 Click the Stop Fitting Text to This Placeholder

> The Year End Results for Fiscal Year 2007 and the plan for year 2008

Formatting Paragraphs

You may want to format the text you have entered by changing its alignment, its indentation, its line spacing, its direction and more. The place to make all these formatting changes is from the Paragraph group which is located on the Home tab.

1 Select the text you want to format

2 Click on the Home tab

3 If you want to increase or decrease the indent level, click the indent buttons

46

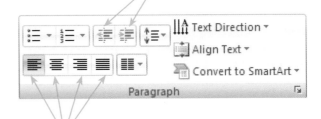

4 Click the alignment buttons to change the alignment or to justify the text

5 If you want to adjust the line spacing you can either click the Line Spacing button and select a value or you can select Line Spacing Options to set your own values

6 Make the adjustments to General, Indentation and Spacing then click on OK to finish

Changing Text Direction

You can change the direction of the text by selecting one of the preset options from the Text Direction menu.

1 Select the text you want to change

2 Click on the Home tab

3 From the Paragraph group click the Text Direction button

4 Select the direction of the text from the available choices

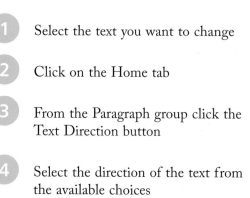

Aligning the Text

1 This time choose the Align Text button from the Paragraph group

2 Select the alignment of the text from the available choices

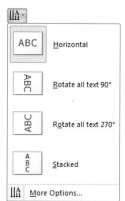

More Options

Once again, you can make adjustments to create a more specific change.

1 From either the Text Direction menu or the Align Text menu select More Options

2 Adjust the settings that are available from this dialog box

3 Click Close

47

Fonts

There are numerous different fonts that you can use in your presentation. You can change the font for a single word, a slide or the whole presentation itself.

Changing the Font on a Single Slide

1 Highlight the word or text you want to change

2 Click on the Home tab if you are not already on it

3 Click on the Font list arrow in the Font group to display all the available fonts

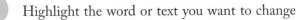

4 Scroll through the list of fonts and select the one you want to use

You will notice that the text you highlighted automatically changes as you scroll through each of the different fonts.

Changing the Font Throughout the Presentation

If you want to change the font throughout your whole presentation, you can access the Slide Master and change the fonts within the theme. Alternatively you can use the Replace Fonts feature of PowerPoint 2007. In order to use this feature you may need to add it to the Quick Access Toolbar.

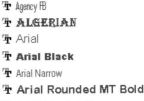

Theme Fonts	
T Calibri	(Headings)
T Calibri	(Body)
All Fonts	
T Agency FB	
T ALGERIAN	
T Arial	
T Arial Black	
T Arial Narrow	
T Arial Rounded MT Bold	
T Arial Unicode MS	
T Baskerville Old Face	
T Bauhaus 93	
T Bell MT	
T Berlin Sans FB	
T Berlin Sans FB Demi	
T Bernard MT Condensed	
T Blackadder ITC	
T Bodoni MT	
T Bodoni MT Black	
T Bodoni MT Condensed	
T Bodoni MT Poster Compressed	
T Book Antiqua	
T Bookman Old Style	

Replace Fonts…

1 Click on the Replace Fonts button

 2 Choose the font you want to replace from the Replace drop-down list

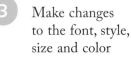

 3 Choose the font you want to replace the font with from the With drop-down list

 4 Click the Replace button

Formatting the Font

You can format any selected text to change the size of the font, the color and even to add various effects, such as strikethrough.

1 Select the text that you want to format

2 Click on the Home tab and then click the Font dialog box launcher

3 Make changes to the font, style, size and color

4 Check any Effects boxes to add the effects to the text

5 Click OK

Hot tip

To add a command to the Quick Access Toolbar, click the right mouse button and select Customize the Quick Access Toolbar and choose All Commands from the Choose commands from drop-down list. Then just select the command you want to add, in this case Replace Fonts, and it will appear on the toolbar.

Hot tip

You can also open the font dialog box by pressing CTRL + SHIFT + F after higlighting the text you want to format.

WordArt

PowerPoint 2007 has a collection of different text styles that you can use in your presentation, which are called WordArt.

Adding WordArt

1 Click the Insert tab

2 Click on the WordArt icon from the Text group

3 Select the WordArt style that you want to use from the available options displayed

Don't forget

You can change the size and rotation of the WordArt text box by using the handles, just as you can do with shapes.

4 A WordArt text box will appear with the words Your Text Here - click on this box to activate it

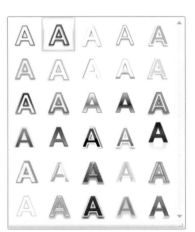

5 Replace the sample text with your own text

6 Move the text box to the correct location on the slide

Formatting WordArt

Once you have added some WordArt you can easily apply formatting to it, including changing the file, the outline and any of the effects.

 1 Click on the WordArt text box to display the Drawing Tools tab

2 Select any of the options from the WordArt Styles group, such as a new style

3 If you click on the down arrow next to either Text Fill or Text Outline, you can choose from a number of additional options, such as color and fill

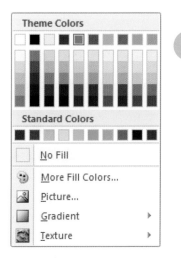

Hot tip

Highlight the effect to see a preview of it on your selected text.

4 If you click on the down arrow next to Text Effects, you can choose from a number of different text effects, such as shadow, glow and reflection

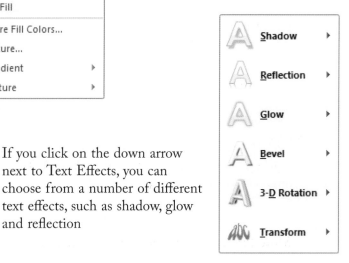

51

...cont'd

5 Highlight the Text Effect you want and then choose from the available options that are displayed depending on the effect you highlighted

6 Repeat for each WordArt text box you want to format

Formatting Text Effects

Text Effects can be easily applied to your WordArt text, which enables you to change the alignment of the text and also the direction.

1 Click on the WordArt text box to display the Drawing Tools tab

2 Click on the Font Text Effects dialog box launcher in the WordArt Styles group

3 Click on the Vertical alignment drop-down list to select a new alignment

4 Click on the Text direction drop-down list to change the direction of the text

5 Click Close

Don't forget

You can change the rotation of the WordArt text box by using the handles, just as you can do with shapes.

52

Find and Replace Text

There may come a time when you might need to either find a text entry in your presentation or even replace some text with something else – for example, a person on your project may have changed and you need to update the presentation to reflect this change so it is not out of date. Instead of having to check each and every slide in your presentation, you can use the Find function, and if you want to replace some text you can then use the Replace function.

1 On the Home tab click Find from the Editing group

> 🔍 Find
> ᵃᵇ₅ₐc Replace ▾
> ↘ Select ▾
> Editing

2 Enter the text in the Find what: box that you want to search for

---

Find ? ✕

Find what:
[   ] ▾   [Find Next]

☐ Match case   [Close]

☐ Find whole words only   [Replace...]

3 Click on Find Next to find the first matching entry

4 If you want to also replace the entry click on Replace

5 Enter the text in the Replace with: box and click Replace

Replace ? ✕

Find what:
[|] ▾   [Find Next]

Replace with:
[   ] ▾   [Close]

☐ Match case   [Replace]

☐ Find whole words only   [Replace All]

Symbols

PowerPoint 2007 comes with a large amount of different types of symbols that you can insert into your presentation. This keeps the presentation looking as professional as possible and to enter freehand text for something such as a trademark symbol.

Hot tip

You can choose the font that you want to use for the symbol by selecting it from the Font drop-down list.

1 Add or click on an existing text box placeholder

2 Click on the Insert tab

3 From the Text group click on Symbol

Hot tip

Rather than searching through all the available symbols you can choose to view a subset, such as Currency Symbols, by selecting from the Subset drop-down list.

4 Scroll through the list of available symbols until you find the symbol that you want to add to your slide

Hot tip

If you use the same symbols on a regular basis you can easily select them from the Recently used symbols group instead of always searching for them.

5 Click on the symbol and then click Insert to add it

Bullets and Numbers

If you want to add a list to your presentation you might want to consider making it a bulleted list or a number list. PowerPoint 2007 provides a number of built-in bullets and numbers lists that you can easily select to make your list look more professional.

1 Select the text you want to add bullets or number to

1 Select the text you want to add bullets or number to

2 Click on the Home tab if it is not already selected

3 From the Paragraph group, select either the Bullets button or the Numbering button

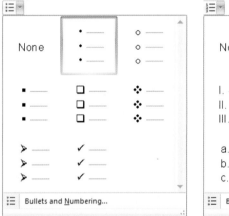

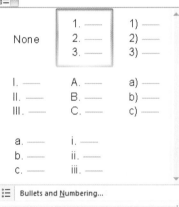

55

4 Click on the required bullet or numbering style

5 If you want to customize the type of bullet or number, click on Bullets and Numbering

6 Click the Bulleted tab to customize Bullets

7 Click the Numbered tab to customize Numbering

Editing Options

Hot tip

The Allow text to be dragged and dropped also enables you to drag and drop text from your PowerPoint presentation to any other Microsoft Office application.

There are a number of advanced options that can be enabled or disabled in order to help you with the way you work with text. These options include:

- When selecting, automatically select entire word – this option will select the entire word when you select any part of the text. The default setting is enabled

- Allow text to be dragged and dropped – this option allows you to drag and drop text anywhere on the screen or to another slide. The default setting is enabled

- Maximum number of undos – this option allows you set the maximum number of times you can use the undo button to rectify mistakes or change what you have done. The default setting is 20 undos and you probably won't need to change it

Hot tip

Using smart cut and paste is very useful as it means your pasted content never runs up against words or objects that are already in place.

- Use smart cut and paste – this option is used to automatically adjust the spacing between words and objects that are pasted into the presentation. The default setting is enabled

1 Click the Microsoft Office Button and then click on Powerpoint Options

2 Click Advanced from the left-hand column

Hot tip

If creating presentations in different languages, it would be a good idea to check the Automatically switch keyboard to match language of surround text box so that the keyboard settings are changed for you rather than you having to go and change them yourself each time.

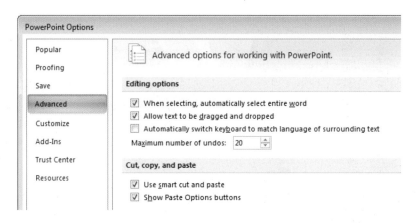

3 Check or uncheck the different settings as required, then click OK to finish

(4) Graphics and Lines

This chapter will tell you how to add various graphics, shapes, lines and arrows. It will also tell you how to edit and format what you have added. It also looks at a new feature of PowerPoint 2007 called SmartArt.

Adding Shapes

PowerPoint 2007 comes with a number of ready-made shapes for you to use in your presentations. These shapes include rectangles, circles, arrows, lines and many others.

1 Click on the Insert tab

2 Click on Shapes from the Illustrations group

58

3 Select the shape you want to add from the list of available shapes

4 You can then just point and click to the area on the slide that you want to add the shape, which will add the shape as a standard size that you can then change

5 You could also choose to hold the left mouse button down on an area of the screen and drag the box until you are happy with the size of the new shape, and when you release the left mouse button the shape will be drawn to that size

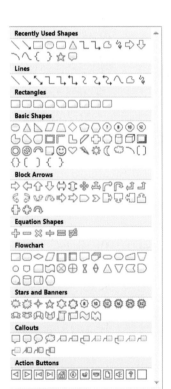

6 If you want to add some text to the shape just click on the shape and type in the text you want to appear within it

Blue circle

Resizing & Adjusting Shapes

You can resize or adjust any shape that you have drawn by using the various handles that will appear when a shape is selected. These handles can appear as green circles, light blue circles and yellow diamonds depending on what their function is.

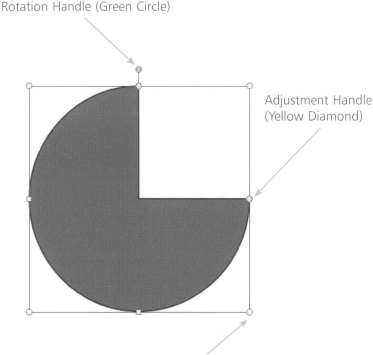

Rotation Handle (Green Circle)

Adjustment Handle (Yellow Diamond)

Sizing Handle (Light Blue Circle)

Hot tip

You might find it easier to zoom in so that you can make precise adjustments to shapes.

Performing Adjustments or Resizing

1 Select the shape you want to resize or adjust

2 To rotate the shape, click and hold the rotation handle

3 To resize the shape, click and hold the sizing handle

4 To adjust the shape, click and hold the adjustment handle

5 Move the mouse until the shape has been resized, rotated or adjusted as required

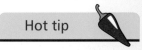

Hot tip

You can select any of the handles of the same type to perform the required adjustments or resizing.

Shape Effects

Another new feature of PowerPoint 2007 is the ability to apply effects to shapes, such as 3-D Rotations, Shadows, Reflections and more. You can apply quick and easy effects using any of the various preset effects or you can select individual effects yourself.

Preset Effects

1 Select the shape you want to set the effect for

2 Click on the Format tab if it is not already highlighted

60

3 From the Shapes Styles group click on Shape Effects

4 Highlight Preset to display the Presets menu

5 Select the Preset you want to use to apply it to the shape

6 You can also remove any preset by clicking on the No Preset option from the list

Individual Effects

If you did not want to use one of the preset effects, maybe because they just were not quite right, then you can choose from a large number of other effects including:

- Shadow – the options include effects for Outer, Inner and Perspective

- Reflection – the option is for Reflection Variations

- Glow – the option is for Glow Variations

- Soft Edges – the options include different point size edges

- Bevel – the option is for different bevel styles

- 3-D Rotation – the options include Parallel, Perspective and Oblique

1 Select the shape you want to set the effect for

2 Click on the Format tab if it is not already highlighted

3 From the Shape Styles group, click on Shape Effects

4 Highlight the effects style you want to select from

5 Select the effect you want to use to apply it to the shape

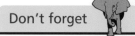

Don't forget

If you highlight an effect you can see a preview of it before you finalize your selection.

Some of the effect styles have additional Options choices, which you can select in order to make some very specific adjustments.

3-D Effects

You can add 3-D effects to any of your shapes by either selecting from the various 3-D effects that are available, or by effectively creating your own by adjusting a number of available settings.

3-D Format Settings

These settings include:

- Bevel – gives an appearance of a raised edge and highlights the edges. You can set the width and height for the raised edge on the top or bottom of the shape

- Depth – used to show distance between the shape and its surface. You can set the color and the depth on the shape

- Contour – used to show a raised border on the whole shape. You can set the color and the size on the shape

- Surface – used to change the material look of the shape, also the level of lighting on the shape as well as the angle of the shape. Choices include special effects, translucent effects, neutral, warm and cool lighting

62

1 Select the shape you want to adjust and click on it

2 Click the Format tab

3 Click on Shape Effects from the Shape Styles group

4 Click on 3-D Format and select Bevel from right of the window

5 Make the necessary changes to the shape

6 Click Close

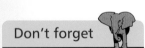
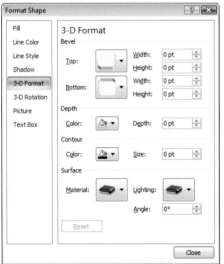

3-D Rotation Settings

These settings include:

- Presets – you can choose from the various presets as you did previously

- Rotation – used to adjust the orientation and position of the shape by adjusting settings for the X axis (horizontal), the Y axis (vertical) and the Z axis (height against other shapes). You can also adjust the perspective of the shape to increase or decrease the foreshortening (the depth dependent growing and shrinking). You can set the perspective between 0 and 120

- Text – used to keep the text flat and prevent it from rotating with the shape

- Object position – used to move the shape backward or forward in 3-D space

1 Select the shape you want to adjust and click on it

2 Click the Format tab

3 Click on Shape Effects from the Shape Styles group

4 Click on 3-D Rotation and select 3-D Rotation Options from the right of the window

5 Make the necessary changes to the shape

6 Click Close

63

SmartArt

SmartArt is a brand new feature that is introduced with PowerPoint 2007. A SmartArt graphic allows you to easily show your information or data without having to create a complex diagram from scratch. Once you have created a SmartArt graphic it is very easy to modify the content plus the look and feel.

There are a number of built-in SmartArt graphics to get you started, including lists, processes, hierachies and relationships. Choosing the right one will depend on what you are trying to show with the graphic, for example you could select Hierarchy if you wanted to create an organizational chart.

You can choose a SmartArt graphic and enter your text or you can convert some of your existing text into a SmartArt graphic.

Create a SmartArt Graphic

1 Click on the Insert tab and select the SmartArt button from the Illustrations group

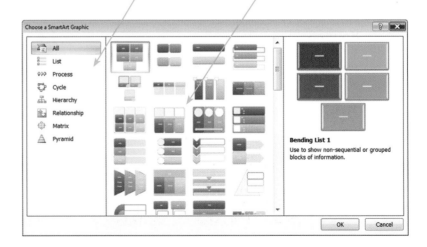

2 Choose the category and then the style of the graphic

Type	Use
List	Show non-sequential information
Process	Shows steps in a process or timeline
Cycle	Shows a continual process
Hierarchy	Used to create an organizational chart or decision tree
Relationship	Illustrates connections
Matrix	Shows how parts relate to a whole
Pyramid	Shows proportional relationships with the largest component on top or bottom

3 Look at the preview to make sure you are happy with your selection and then click OK

4 Enter the text in the relevant [Text] boxes to see it displayed in your chosen graphic

5 Click outside of the graphic to finish

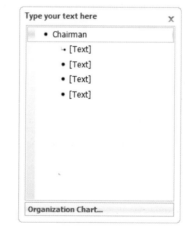

Hot tip

If the text entry box is not displayed, click on the tab with the arrows to the left of the SmartArt graphic image.

65

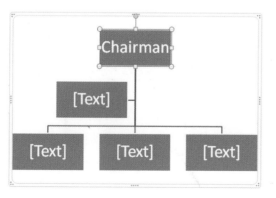

Modifying SmartArt

Now that you have created your SmartArt graphic you can modify it to suit your presentation. These modifications can include changing the layout, the style, the color and more as you need.

Changing the Layout

You can easily select a different layout by selecting one from the group of Layouts that are available to you.

Don't forget

You can see a preview of the change by hovering over a layout from the layouts box or a style from the SmartArt Styles box, this means that you don't have to make the change to see what it will look like.

1 Select the SmartArt graphic you want to change

2 Ensure the Design tab is active under SmartArt Tools

3 In the Layouts box select the new layout or click on the More arrow button to show additional layouts

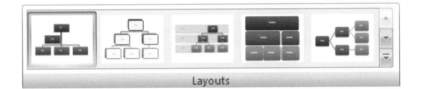

Layouts

Changing the Style

You can easily select a different style by selecting one from the group of Quick Styles that are available to you.

1 Select the SmartArt graphic you want to change

2 Ensure the Design tab is active under SmartArt Tools

3 In the SmartArt Styles box select the new style or click on the More arrow button to show additional styles

SmartArt Styles

4 If you want to change the color variation that is applied to the SmartArt graphic, click on the Change Colors button

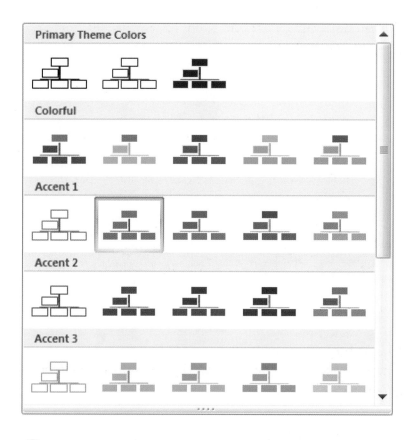

 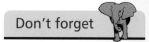
5 Scroll through the list of colors and select the one that matches your requirement

Resetting a SmartArt Graphic

If you make a mistake or you change your mind, it is very easy to reset the graphic back to its original look before the change.

1 From the Design tab click the Reset button

Reset
Graphic

Reset

Converting to SmartArt

You don't have to create the SmartArt graphic and then enter your text. If you already have some text on a slide you can easily convert it to a SmartArt graphic with the click of the mouse.

 1 Select the text placeholder on the slide that you want to convert to a SmartArt graphic so that it is highlighted

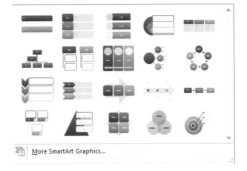

Hot tip

You can also convert the text into a SmartArt graphic by first selecting the text box and then clicking the right mouse button and selecting Convert to SmartArt from the context menu.

2 Click the Convert to SmartArt icon from the Paragraph group on the Home tab

3 Select the SmartArt graphic layout that you want to use for your slide (you can also click the More SmartArt Graphics button to see more)

Don't forget

If you are not happy with the way the SmartArt graphic appears, you can either change it or press the Undo button on the Quick Access Toolbar to revert the text back to its original state.

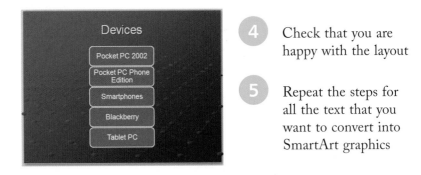

4 Check that you are happy with the layout

5 Repeat the steps for all the text that you want to convert into SmartArt graphics

68

Ruler and Gridlines

To make the positioning of placeholders and other objects easier you can display a ruler and also display gridlines.

 1 Click on the View tab

2 From the Show/Hide group click Ruler to display the Ruler, and click Gridlines to display Gridlines

The Slide Pane with the Ruler Displayed

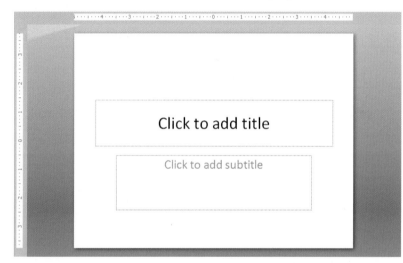

Click to add title

Click to add subtitle

The Slide Pane with Gridlines Displayed

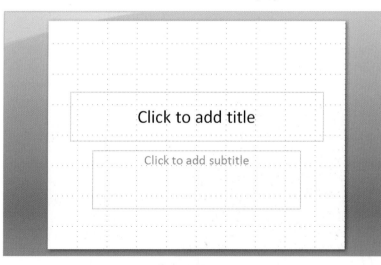

Click to add title

Click to add subtitle

Arrangements

There might come a time when you want to change the arrangements of either your shapes, pictures, text or other objects within your presentations. These arrangement changes could be changing the position, rotating or flipping them or changing the order of a group of objects.

Rotating and Flipping Objects

Don't forget

You can rotate an object by using the rotation handle.

① Select the object you want to rotate or flip

② Click on the Format tab

③ Click on Rotate from the Arrange group

④ Click on Rotate to rotate the object either 90 degrees left or right

⑤ Click on Flip to flip the object vertically or horizontally

Changing Object Sizes

You can change the size of an object in many different ways. One of the quickest ways is to alter the figures in the Size group.

Don't forget

You can also change an object size by using the sizing handle.

① Click on the object you want to resize and click the Format tab

② Enter the new Height and Width in the Size group

Changing Object Position

You can change the position of any object, for example, bringing it forward or moving it back in comparison to any another object.

① Select the object you want to change the position of

② Click on the Format tab

③ Select Bring to Front from the Arrange group

Selection Pane

Sometimes it would be easier to work on a slide if some of the objects were not there. You can easily hide and then show any object that is on a slide to make it easier for you to work and even to layer objects into your presentation.

① Click on any object on the slide

② Click on the Format tab

③ Click on Selection Pane from the Arrange group

④ Click on any listed object to highlight it on the slide

⑤ If you want to hide the object click on the Eye icon

⑥ To show the hidden object again click on the Eye icon once more

Selection and Visibility ▼ ✕

Shapes on this Slide:

TextBox 6

Oval 5

Oval 4

Show All ⬆ ⬇

Hide All Re-order

Hot tip

You should consider using the selection pane if some of the objects on the slide are not easily accessible.

71

Lines and Arrows

Most presentations will at some point include a line or an arrow. It is very easy to add a simple line and then format it to suit your purposes, which can also include adding arrow heads to the line.

Drawing a Line

1 Click on the Home tab or the Insert tab

2 Click the Shapes button in the Drawing group

3 Select a Line or Arrow shape from the available list

4 Click and drag the mouse pointer to add the line to your presentation (you can make the line as long as you want and whichever angle you want as well)

5 Release the mouse button to draw the line

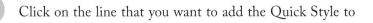

Adding a Quick Style to a Line

1 Click on the line that you want to add the Quick Style to

2 Click on the Home tab

3 Click on the Quick Styles button from the Drawing group

4 Highlight the style you want to use and check that it looks OK on your slide

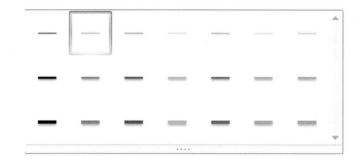

5　If you are happy with the way the new style looks, click on the style to make the change

6　Repeat the steps for each line you want to add a Quick Style to

Adding Arrows to Lines

1　Click on the line that you want to add the arrow to

2　Click on the Format tab

3　Click on the Shape Outline button from the Shape Styles group

4　Click on the Arrows button

73

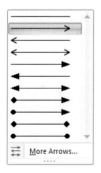

5　Click on the Arrow type that you want to use to add to your line

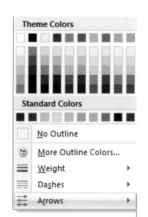

6　Repeat the steps for each line you want to add an arrow to

...cont'd

Modifying a Line

1 Click on the Line that you want to modify and click on the Format tab

2 Click on the Shape Outline button from the Shape Styles group

3 To change the thickness of the line click on Weight

4 Choose the thickness you want to apply to your line

5 To change the style of the line click on Dashes

6 Choose the style of the line you want to apply to your line

Formatting a Line

You can also make formatting changes to the lines.

1 Select the line you want to format and click the Format tab

2 Click the Format Shape dialog box launcher from the Shape Styles group

3 Adjust the various settings as you need and click Close

Freeforms and Scribbles

Within the available choices in the Lines box, there are two additional choices – Freeform and Scribble. Both can be used to create customized lines or shapes. You would use Freeform if you wanted to create a shape that has both curved and straight segments and you would use Scribble if you wanted to create a line or shape that looked like it was drawn by hand with a pen.

Freeforms – Straight Lines

1 Click on the Home or Insert tab

2 Click on Shapes and select the Freeform icon from Lines

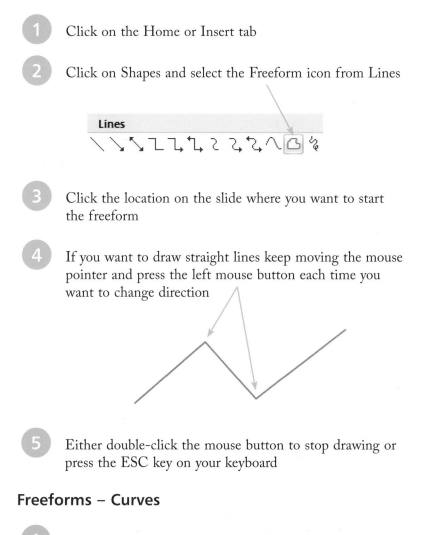

3 Click the location on the slide where you want to start the freeform

4 If you want to draw straight lines keep moving the mouse pointer and press the left mouse button each time you want to change direction

5 Either double-click the mouse button to stop drawing or press the ESC key on your keyboard

Freeforms – Curves

1 To draw curves just repeat steps 1 through 3 above, only this time hold down the mouse button and drag the mouse to draw

Hot tip

Once you have drawn the line or shape, you can easily change the weight, color and other properties by selecting what you want to change and clicking on the Format tab.

...cont'd

2 Release the mouse button when you have finished

Freeforms – Filled Shapes

1 To draw a filled shape, repeat steps 1 through 3 from the Straight Lines section

2 Using a combination of holding the mouse button down to draw straight lines and releasing the mouse button to draw curves, draw the shape you want to appear

3 To complete the shape and fill it in automatically you must join the last point to the first point

Scribbles

1 Click on the Home or Insert tab

2 Click on Shapes and select the Scribble icon from Lines

Lines

3 Click and hold the mouse button on the start point

4 Drag the mouse pointer across the slide, drawing your shape

5 Release the mouse button

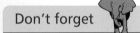

Don't forget

You can also create a filled scribble by joining up the start and end points of the scribble, just as you did for a filled freeform shape.

5 Tables and Charts

This chapter will explain some of the table and chart options provided by PowerPoint 2007, including the ability to use Excel 2007 functionality.

Tables

Tables have been greatly enhanced in PowerPoint 2007, for example, it is now much easier to reuse a table that you already have in Word 2007 or Excel 2007.

Adding a Table

There are a number of ways to add a table to your presentation.

 Click the Insert tab on the toolbar

 Click Table

Hot tip

Because there are a number of different ways to add a table to your presentation, it will most likely come down to whichever method you are most comfortable with using so, make sure you try all the different ways to get a feel for it.

Insert Table

Insert Table...

Draw Table

Excel Spreadsheet

3 Highlight the number of rows and columns that you want to represent your table (such as 2 down and 5 across) then click the mouse button to add the table to the slide

That is not the only way to add a new table into your presentation there are some others that you could use.

Inserting a Table

 Click the Insert tab on the toolbar

Click Table

Click Insert Table from the bottom of the Insert Table section

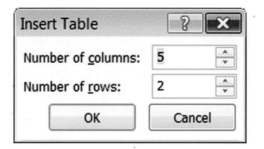

Hot tip

To add an additional row at the end of your table, click on the last cell in the last row and press the TAB button on your keyboard.

79

Enter the number of required columns and rows for the table

 Click OK to add the table to the slide

Inserting a Table on a New Slide

There is also another way of adding a new table to a slide. If you are creating a new slide and the slide layout include a set of icons for adding either tables, charts, graphics and others, you can simply click on the table icon to launch the Insert Table dialog box.

Table Styles and Layouts

Once you have created your table, you can apply different styles to it, change the borders, change the colors and more.

Table styles are a combination of different formatting options, including colors which are determined by the theme colors of your presentation. To change the style:

1 Select the table you want to change styles

2 Under Table Tools on the Design tab choose a style from the thumbnailed Table Styles group

Table Styles

3 Click on Table Effects to add an effect, such as a shadow or reflection

Cell Bevel ▶

Shadow ▶

Reflection ▶

4 Click on Shading to change either the theme colors or the standard colors

Theme Colors

Standard Colors

More Border Colors...

5 If you only want to change a specific part of the table, use the Quick Style Options group

☐ Header Row   ☐ First Column
☐ Total Row   ☐ Last Column
☐ Banded Rows   ☐ Banded Columns

Quick Style Options

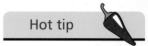

6 Click on the Borders button to bring up the various border options that you can change, for example, adding or removing borders from certain cells

7 You can change the individual cell size by either dragging the cell to the size you want or by entering the new height and width sizes in the Cell Size group

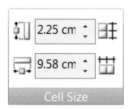

Hot tip

To merge cells together, highlight those cells and click the Merge Cells button in the Merge group. To split merged cells, just click on the Split Cells button.

Rows and Columns

If you need to, you can add or remove rows and columns, or even merge cells together, or split cells up.

1 Click on the cell above or below the row you want to add or, the left or right of a column

2 Click on the Layout tab, under Table Tools, go to the Rows & Columns group

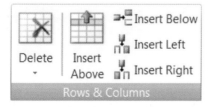

Hot tip

To delete a row or a column, highlight what you want to delete and either use the Delete option from the Rows & Columns group or press the BACKSPACE key on your keyboard. If you just want to delete the contents of the cell press DEL on your keyboard.

3 Click on the button that represents what and where you want to add, for example, click Insert Above if you want the row to be added above your current cell position

81

Drawing a Table

You an also add a table by drawing its borders and changing its design and layout by hand.

1. Click the Insert tab on the toolbar

2. Click Table

3. Click Draw Table from the bottom of the Insert Table section

4. The pointer will change into a pencil, you then click and drag a box to the size you want the table in order to draw the border of a table. You can also continue to draw lines with the pencil within the border to add columns and rows

5. If you make a mistake and add a line, you can easily remove it by selecting the Eraser. This changes the pointer to an eraser and you only have to click on a line to remove it

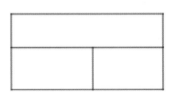

6. You can also change the border type, the line thickness and the color of the pen used from this group

7. If you need to change the size of the table, enter the new height and width on the Table Size group

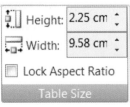

Chart Types

PowerPoint 2007 supports a large number of different types of charts, including pie charts, bar charts, line charts, and many more.

The following is a very brief description of some of the available chart types to help you decide which might be the right one for your presentation:

Column

Column charts are useful for showing changes in data over periods of time and are useful for showing comparisons between data.

Line

Line charts are useful for displaying data over periods of time and displaying trends in that data.

Pie

Pie charts show the data as a percentage of the whole in segments and are used to display statistics.

Bar

Bar charts use vertical or horizontal bars to show comparisons among two or more items.

Area

Each area is given a solid color or pattern to emphasize the relationships between the pieces of charted information.

Stock

This chart is useful if you want to easily display stock prices.

Doughnut

This chart is very similar to a pie chart but contains more than one data series.

Radar

Radar charts are used to compare the aggregate values of a number of data series.

Hot tip

Each chart type has a number of different subtypes available to select from, including 3-D charts.

Hot tip

For more detailed descriptions of all the available chart types, including examples, check out the Help function in PowerPoint and search for available chart types.

Adding Charts

Once you have decided on what type of chart you want to use, adding it to your presentation is very simple.

 1 Click on the Insert tab

2 From the Illustrations group, click on Chart

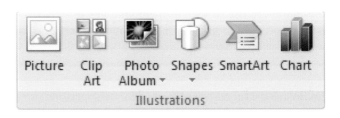

3 Click on the chart type you want to use

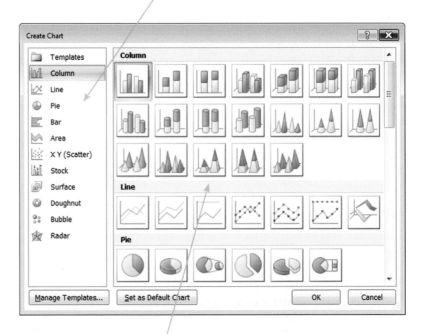

4 Click on the chart subtype you want to use

5 Click OK to create the new chart

6 Enter the data you want, and change any of the data labels that appear in the sample

	A	B
1	Column1	Emails Sent
2	1st Qtr	45
3	2nd Qtr	28
4	3rd Qtr	79
5	4th Qtr	34

Hot tip

If you have Excel 2007, make sure it is installed so that PowerPoint 2007 uses this for the data entry and manipulation. If you don't have Excel, Microsoft Graph is used instead.

7 Close Excel and your chart will be updated in PowerPoint

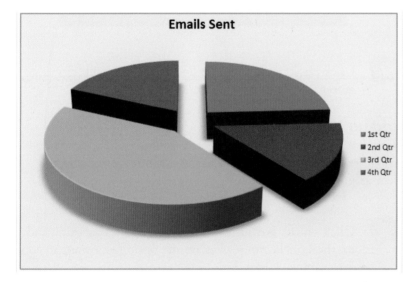

85

Don't forget

If you want to use the data again, make sure you save the Excel worksheet.

8 If you want to use a different type of chart, you can easily change it by clicking on the Change Chart Type button in the type group and selecting a different chart type

9 Add any text or graphics that you want to use with the chart

Enhancing the Charts

You can do a lot to enhance the look of your charts. This section will give you an introduction to what is available in PowerPoint.

Chart Styles
There are numerous different styles you can choose from for your chart, ranging from standard flat charts to full color 3-D charts.

 Highlight the chart you want to enhance and on the Chart Styles menu, choose a new style from the ones available

 Click on your chosen style and your chart will automatically be updated to reflect the new style

Adding Labels and Titles
Now that your chart has been created, you can add a legend and any other labels you need to make the meaning of the chart as clear as possible.

Hot tip

Make sure your labels and legends are clear and concise – you don't want to take away from the impact of the chart.

 Click on the Layout tab under the Chart Tools title and on the Labels group, click on the option you want to add, for example, Chart Title

 Choose the title option you want to use and enter the title for the chart

Axes and Gridlines

Depending on your chart type, you can display or hide both axes and gridlines.

1 Click on the Layout tab under the Chart Tools title

2 On the Axes group, click either the Axes button or the Gridlines button and make a selection from the available options. For example, if you want to display an axis, click on the type of axis you want to display and then choose one of the options

Changing the Format of Elements

You can change the format of individual elements of your chart or the whole chart itself.

1 Click on the Format tab under the Chart Tools title

2 On the Current Selection group, click on the arrow to choose the element you want to select

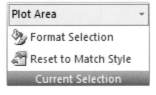

3 Click on Format Selection

4 Make any changes you want, if you make a mistake or want to go back, click the Reset to Match Style button

Changing or Showing the Data

If you should decide to change the data at any time, or you want to show the data, you can by choosing the relevant option from the Data group.

1 Click on the required icon from the Data tab to see or edit the source data

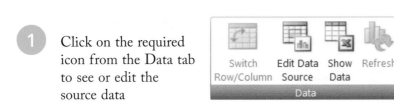

Using Excel 2007

Excel Charts

When you copy a chart that you have created in Excel 2007 and paste it into PowerPoint 2007, the chart data is then linked with the Excel worksheet. If you want to update the data at anytime, you must update the Excel worksheet which in turn updates the chart in PowerPoint.

1. In Excel, make sure you have already created the chart and then select the chart by clicking the border and selecting Copy from the Clipboard group

2. Go to your PowerPoint presentation

3. Click on Paste from the Clipboard group to paste the Excel chart onto your slide

Copying Excel Tables

You can easily create a new Excel table in PowerPoint or you can copy and paste an existing table directly from Excel.

Don't forget

You must have Excel 2007 installed in order to add an Excel table into PowerPoint 2007, to take advantage of the advanced charting capabilities.

1. In Excel, make sure you have already created the table and then select the table by clicking the border and selecting Copy from the Clipboard group

2. Go to your PowerPoint presentation

3. Click on Paste from the Clipboard group to paste the Excel table onto your slide

Inserting Excel Tables

If you have not yet created your table in Excel, you can create it directly in PowerPoint.

Hot tip

You can also copy or link in charts and tables direct from Word 2007 in the same way as Excel 2007.

1. Click the Insert tab on the toolbar and click Table

2. Click on Excel Spreadsheet to add a blank Excel table

6 Enhancing Presentations

This chapter will tell you how to enhance your presentation using very simple but effective options.

Themes

If you want to give your presentation a professional look and feel without having to spend a considerable amount of time formatting it, you could use one of PowerPoint's many themes.

A theme includes specific colors and fonts, and also effects.

You can even create your own themes if there is not one that suits your needs and you can then reuse it later.

Applying a Theme

 Click on the Design tab

 In the Themes group, click on the More button to reveal all of the available themes

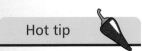 Click on the theme that you want to use

As you can see from the examples below, just by selecting a different theme, your presentation can be dramatically different.

Themes can be applied to an entire presentation or to individual slides, the choice is entirely yours. You can even set a theme to be the default. Right-click the theme for these options.

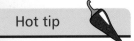

Hot tip

When you hover over a theme your presentation will change to give you a preview of the theme. If you like the theme, click it to make the change, if you don't like it, just carry on previewing.

Hot tip

You can search for additional themes online by clicking on the Search Office Online option in the themes list.

Effects

Theme effects are collections of lines and fills that are part of each theme. Unlike colors and fonts, you cannot create your own effects, however, you can select which effect you want to use in your theme.

 In the Themes group, click on the Effects button to display the effects list

■ Colors ▾
A Fonts ▾
● Effects ▾

② Scroll through the effects list and click on the effect you wish to use for your theme

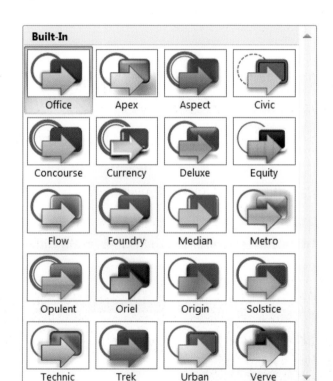

Built-In

Office	Apex	Aspect	Civic
Concourse	Currency	Deluxe	Equity
Flow	Foundry	Median	Metro
Opulent	Oriel	Origin	Solstice
Technic	Trek	Urban	Verve

As you can see, each effect is slightly different so it may be a case of trial and error choosing between them until you find one that suits your presentation.

Customizing Themes

You can change the colors, the fonts, and the line and fill effects that are used for a specific theme. You can then immediately use that changed theme or save it as a custom theme so that you can use it again later in a different presentation.

Theme Colors

Each theme contains four text and background colors, six accent colors, and two hyperlink colors. The four colors in the square buttons are the current text and background colors, the eight colored squares that appear in the color list represent the accent colors and hyperlink colors in that order.

1   In the Themes group, click on the Colors button to display the colors list

2   Scroll through the colors list and click on the Create New Theme Colors button

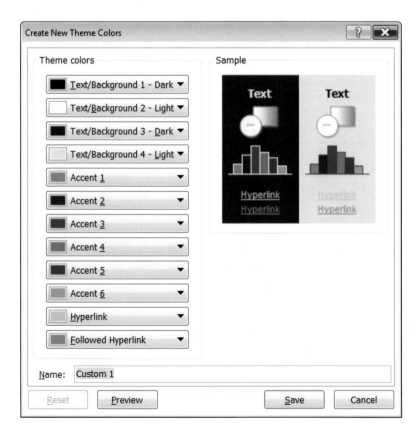

3 Click on the boxes next to each color option and select the new color you want to use for that option

4 Enter a name for your new custom theme and click Save

Theme Fonts

Each theme font contains a heading and a body font, and these can both be different fonts if you wish.

1 In the Themes group, click on the Fonts button to display the colors list

2 Scroll through the colors list and click on the Create New Theme Fonts button

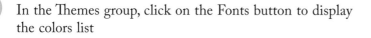

3 Select the fonts you want to use for both the Heading and the Body

4 Enter a name for your new custom font and click Save

Don't forget

If you want to reset the theme colors back to their original settings, click on the Reset button before you click Save.

Hot tip

Save your new theme so that you can apply it to any other presentation in the future. Click on the More button and then click Save Current Theme.

Animations

You can add animations to a number of different elements in your presentation, including text, sounds, graphics, SmartArt diagrams and more. This can help to greatly enhance the presentation and is quick and easy to do, leaving you more time to concentrate on the content.

You can use one of the built-in animations or you can create your own and you can apply the animations to the whole slide or to different elements so that each element could have a different effect.

The animations also have specific effects associated with them.

You can also add slide transitions to enhance the effect even more. We will cover slide transitions later.

1 Highlight the word, letter, or whatever object you want to animate

2 Click on the Animations tab and in the Animations group click on the Animate list to see the available animations depending on the object you chose

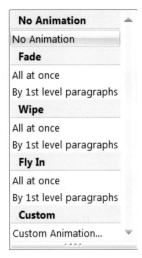

3 Choose the effect from the list of Fades, Wipes or Fly Ins and you will be shown a short preview of what the animation will look like

4 Choose any other objects you want to add effects to and repeat the above steps

5 If you want to see what the whole thing then looks like, click the Preview button

Custom Animations

You use custom animations when you want to control exactly what happens and when.

1 Highlight the word, letter, or whatever object you want to animate

2 Click on the Animations tab and in the Animations group click on the Custom Animation button

3 Click the Add Effect button to list the available effects

4 Click on the type of effect you want to add, for example, highlight Motion Paths if you want to create your own path for the object

5 Choose the path you want to use or highlight Draw Custom Path and select the type of custom path, for example, Curve

6 Click on the start point with your mouse and move around the screen, clicking on each point and pressing Enter when you are finished to see a preview of the animation

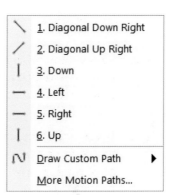

Hot tip

You can view your entire presentation by clicking the Slide Show button at the bottom of the Custom Animation box.

...cont'd

Each effect you add will be numbered and you can see the start point, path and end point for each effect by the number appearing on the slide.

Hot tip

You can change the sequence in which the effects appear by using the up and down arrows next to Re-Order.

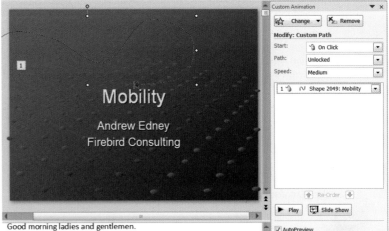

Good morning ladies and gentlemen.

Hot tip

Use Timings to make the presentation look even more professional (instead of clicking on objects). Using timings is also beneficial when you create self-running presentations.

7 For each animation, you can select how it starts, its path and the speed it will go from the menu

8 You can even add sound to the animation by right-clicking the animation in the list and selecting Effect Options

9 Make any changes you want to the Effect, the Timing, and the Text Animation, and click on OK

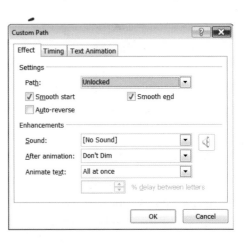

Animating SmartArt

You can add animations to your SmartArt graphics or to individual shapes in your SmartArt graphic.

As with other animations, the actual animations that are available will depend on the layout you selected for your SmartArt graphic. The animations you can apply to SmartArt graphics are different from the animations that you may have applied to other objects.

These differences include:

- The connecting lines between each of the shapes are always associated with the second shape and are not animated individually

- Animations will appear in the order that the shapes in the SmartArt graphics appear. You can reverse the order but you cannot change the sequence unless you create multiple slides

1 Highlight the SmartArt graphic you want to animate

2 Click on the Animations tab and in the Animations group click on the Animate list to see the animations

The available animations include:

- As one object – the SmartArt graphic is treated as though it was a single object rather than multiple objects

- All at once – all the shapes in the SmartArt graphic are animated simultaneously. This is different to the As one object animation in which the entire object is animated as a single object

- One by one – each shape is animated one at a time

- By branch one by one – all the shapes in the same branch are animated one at a time

- By level at once – all the shapes in the same branch are animated at the same time

- By level one by one – all the shapes are animated first by level and then individually within the level

Beware

Even though you can apply a different animation to any part of the SmartArt graphic, try not to use too many as it can detract from the presentation rather than enhance it!

Beware

Beware when running a Macro – make sure you know what it is doing and where it is from. See the Security chapter later in the book for more information on Macros.

Hot tip

You can also add an action to an existing object or piece of text, highlighting it and clicking on the Action button in the Links group.

Hot tip

Use the Custom action button to define your own shape – you can pretty much make it look like anything you want.

Actions

An action button can be used in your presentation to perform a function, such as linking to something or even running a separate program or macro.

Action buttons can be predefined buttons, shapes and arrows – for example, if you wanted an action button to be used to move to the next slide in a self-running presentation, you could use a right arrow to perform this function for you.

Adding an Action Button

You can add action buttons that activate the action when they are clicked or even when they have the mouse go over them.

 1 Click the Insert tab and click on the More arrow in the Shapes Group

2 Scroll down to the Action Buttons group of icons

Action Buttons

There are a number of predefined action buttons you can select from, including forward and back, information, movie, sound or even custom. These buttons do not have any actions associated with them, but they are useful for using if you don't want to have to create something new.

3 Click on the action button you want to add

4 Click and drag onto the slide to add the action button and launch the Action Settings dialog box

5 If you want the action to be performed when you click the button, ensure the Mouse Click tab is active. If you want the action to be performed when the pointer moves over the button, click on the Mouse Over tab

Action Settings

Mouse Click | Mouse Over

Action on click

- ● None
- ○ Hyperlink to:
  - Next Slide ▼
- ○ Run program:
  - [   ] Browse...
- ○ Run macro:
  - [   ] ▼
- ○ Object action:
  - [   ] ▼

☐ Play sound:
  - [No Sound] ▼
☐ Highlight click

OK | Cancel

Don't forget

The Macro and Object settings are only available if your presentation contains either a macro or an OLE object.

6 Click on the button that represents the action you want to be performed, for example, if you want to link to another slide, click the Hyperlink to button

7 Choose the slide to link to, or browse for the program to run, if that was what you selected

8 Click OK

The action button will then appear on the screen and you can change the size and shape, or add text to it by double-clicking on the button and choosing from the format options.

Hot tip

Add sounds to the action to enhance the presentation.

Hyperlinks

A hyperlink is used to link a piece of text or an object, such as a picture, to something else, such as another slide in the presentation, a slide in a different presentation, a file, a web page or even an email address, depending on what you need the link for.

Link to Another Slide in Your Presentation

1 Select the text or the object you want to use as the link

2 Click on the Insert tab and then click on the Hyperlink button in the Links group to launch the Edit Hyperlink dialog box

Hot tip

Use the Screen Tip button to add some text that will appear when you hover over the linked object or text – such as a description of what it will link to.

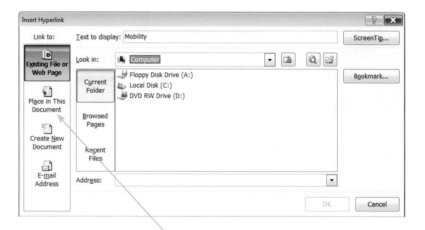

3 Click on the Place in This Document button and then choose the slide from the list of available slides to go to when the link is clicked and then click OK to finish

5 If you chose a piece of text it will appear with a line underneath it. Click the text to activate the link

6 You can edit, open, copy or remove the link by right-clicking on the link

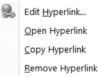

Create a Link to an E-mail Address

 Click on the E-mail Address button from the Edit Hyperlink dialog box

E-mail address:

| |

Subject:

| |

 Enter the e-mail address you want to send to and also enter a Subject for the message, and then click OK

Link to a Slide in a Different Presentation
You can even link to a slide that can be found in a completely different presentation.

 Click on the Existing File or Web Page button from the Edit Hyperlink dialog box

 Click on the presentation you want to use the slide from

 Click on the Bookmark button

 Scroll through the list of slides in the presentation you have selected and click on the one you want to link to

 Click OK

Don't forget

If you create a link to something and you later move that something, make sure you update the link or it won't work!

101

Select Place in Document

Select an existing place in the document:

- First Slide
- Last Slide
- Next Slide
- Previous Slide
- Slide Titles
  - 1. Mobility
  - 2. Agenda
  - 3. Devices
  - 4. Windows Powered Devices
  - 5. Slide 5
  - 6. Smartphone
  - 7. Slide 7
  - 8. Orange SPV Smartphone
  - 9. Orange SPVx Smartphone
  - 10. Slide 10
  - 11. Mobility Solutions
  - 12. Slide 12
  - 13. Mobile Information Server 2002

OK   Cancel

Headers and Footers

Headers and Footers are there to enable you to add information to your slides, handouts and notes. This information can include:

- The date and/or time
- The slide number
- Titles, for example, the title of the presentation
- And much more

Adding a Footer to a Slide

1 Click on the Insert tab

2 Click the Header and Footer icon from the Text group

Hot tip

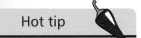

Slides by default do not contain headers, however, you can move a footer to be a header quite easily.

Hot tip

When you check something to include on the slide, the preview window will highlight where the item will be displayed on the slide.

Header and Footer	? X

Slide | Notes and Handouts

Include on slide

☐ Date and time

 ○ Update automatically

 9/11/2006

  Language: Calendar type:

  English (U.S.) Western

 ◉ Fixed

☐ Slide number

☐ Footer

☐ Don't show on title slide

Apply to All

Apply

Cancel

Preview

3 Check the Footer box and enter the text you want

4 Click Apply for that slide, or Apply to All for all slides

5 If you want to add the date and time, or the slide number to the slides, check the relevant boxes

Adding Headers and Footers to Handouts & Notes

1 Click on the Insert tab

2 Click the Header and Footer icon from the Text group

3 Click on the Notes and Handouts tab

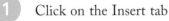

Header and Footer

Slide | Notes and Handouts

Include on page

☐ Date and time

◉ Update automatically

9/11/2006

Language: English (U.S.)   Calendar type: Western

○ Fixed

9/11/2006

☐ Header

☑ Page number

☐ Footer

Apply to All

Cancel

Preview

Hot tip

You can change the position of the header and footers on the slide, and also the font, color and other attributes, by editing the slide master as mentioned in an earlier chapter.

103

4 Check the boxes for what you want to include

5 If you want to add the date and time, or the slide number to the slides, check the relevant boxes

6 Click Apply to All

Background Styles

Background styles are used along with the themes and effects to make your presentation look just that little bit more professional. A background style is created from a combination of theme colors and the currently selected document theme.

Add a Background Style

In earlier versions of PowerPoint, you needed a design template to set a background. In PowerPoint 2007 you add a background style.

1 Click on the Design tab

2 Click on the Background Styles button from the Background group to display a list of available styles

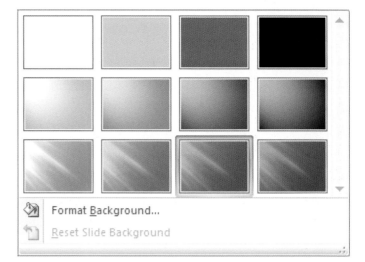

Hover over the background style to preview your slides with that style.

104

Make your presentation handouts easier to read by hiding background objects. To do this, place a check in the Hide Background Graphics box in the Background group.

3 When you have decided on which style to choose, right-click and then click Apply to Select Slides (if you have selected individual slides to change) or click on Apply to All Slides to have the new style applied throughout your presentation

You can also customize a background style by clicking on the Format Background button and then changing the options to suit the background as you see fit.

7 Multimedia Experience

This chapter will tell you about the different multimedia options available in PowerPoint and how to use them to your advantage.

Adding Movies

Movies can be used to enhance your presentation and can be added from either files on your computer, or from the clip organizer (which will be covered later in this chapter).

Adding movies from files on your computer

1 Go to the slide where you want to add the movie or movies

2 Click on the Insert tab and click on the arrow under Movie from the Media Clips menu

3 Click on Movie from File

4 Select the Movie you want to add

5 Choose how you want the movie to start in the slide show

A still image of the start of the movie will then appear on the slide. Change the size of the movie box and the location of the box where appropriate.

Adding Flash Movies

You can also add Macromedia Flash movies to your presentations, although this is not quite as easy as adding other movie files.

The Flash movie needs to be saved as a Shockwave file with a .swf extension for this to work. Also, you will need to add an ActiveX control to PowerPoint.

1 Click on the Microsoft Office Button and select PowerPoint Options

2 From the Personalize menu, put a check in the Show Developer tab in the Ribbon box

3 Click on the newly added Developer tab and then click on the More Controls button

4 Scroll through the control options and click on Shockwave Flash Object and then click OK

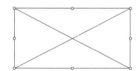

5 Drag your pointer over the slide to add a control box (this is where the Shockwave file will be added). Resize and move it if required

6 Right-click the control box and click on Properties

7 Scroll down until you see the Movie property box on the Alphabetic tab

8 In the value column, enter the full path to the file, including the file name

9 To play the file automatically change the Playing property to True

Movie Options

Once you have placed the movie onto a slide in your presentation, you have a number of options available to you.

The options include:

- Changing the volume
- When to play the movie
- Playing the movie full screen

1 Click the movie you want to change the options for to activate the Movie Options menu

	Play Movie	When Clicked ▾	Loop Until Stopped
Slide Show Volume ▾	Hide During Show		Rewind Movie After Playing
	Play Full Screen		

Movie Options

2 Change any of the settings as required, for example, if you want to play the movie when it is clicked, choose When Clicked from the Play Movie dialog box

Arrangements

You can easily change the arrangement of the movie file on your slide, for example, by rotating it or changing its position relative to the other items on the slide (such as behind or in front of something else).

1 Click the movie you want to activate the Arrange menu

Bring to Front ▾	Send to Back ▾	Selection Pane	Align ▾	Group ▾	Rotate ▾

Arrange

2 Select whichever arrangement option you want to use

Size and Position

You may not want to play the movie full screen during your presentation and so you have the option to resize it.

When you resize a movie, the aspect ratio may change and the movie may appear squashed or out of shape. To keep the aspect ratio the same, select the Lock aspect ratio check box.

1 Click the movie you want to change the size of and either adjust the height and the width to whatever size you want, or to have more options, click on the arrow to launch the Size and Position dialog box

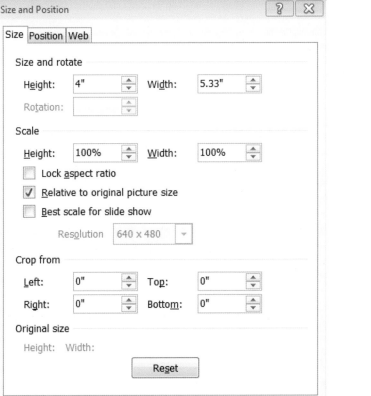

You can have PowerPoint scale the movie file for you to fit the resolution of the presentation, by using the Best scale for slide show check box and selecting your resolution. This will also help to prevent the movie from skipping if it is sized incorrectly.

If you make a mistake, just click on the Reset button.

2 Make any changes and click on Close

Adding Sounds

Sounds can be used to enhance your presentation and can be added from a number of different sources:

- From files on your computer
- From the clip organizer
- Directly from a CD
- By recording your own sounds

Adding Sounds from Files on your Computer

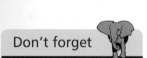

1 Go to the slide where you want to add the sound or sounds

2 Click on the Insert tab and click on the arrow under Sound from the Media Clips menu

3 Click on Sound from File

4 Select the sound you want to add

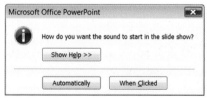

5 Choose how you want the sound to start in the slide show

An icon that looks like a speaker will then appear on the slide. Move this icon to an appropriate position.

You can preview your sound by clicking on the preview button.

110

Sound Options

If you click on any of the speaker icons in your presentation, you will gain access to the SoundTools Options menu.

Within the sound options menu, you can change the slide show volume, have the sound play continuously until its stopped, change how the sound is played, hide the sound icon, or even set the maximum sound file size.

Embedded and Linked Sounds

You can choose to embed or link a sound into your presentation, depending on the type of sound file you want to use.

Embedded sounds are those that are contained within your presentation, and are saved with it, and linked sounds are those that are outside of your presentation.

Using linked sounds is useful for a number of reasons, including that it keeps the size of your presentation down and also if you update the source sound file, the presentation is automatically updated.

By default, the maximum sound file size that can be embedded is 100 KB. You can change this setting to anything up to 50,000 KB (50 megabytes).

However, the larger the embedded sound file, the larger your presentation will become.

You can change the size by changing the number in Max Sound File Size box in the Sound Options menu, but this only effects any sound files you add from that point on, if you have any existing sound files you must delete them and re-add them in order to use the larger size.

Beware

Only choose the Hide During Show option to hide the sound icon if you have set the sound to start automatically, otherwise you will not be able to start the sound!

Hot tip

Why not copy the sound files you want to use to the same folder as your presentation? That way the sounds and the presentation will always be together.

Sounds from Other Sources

Playing Music from a CD

You can add music from your favorite CDs and have it play during your presentation. You can also have the music playing before or after your presentation to give your audience something to listen to.

1 Insert the CD into the CD drive of your computer

2 Select the slide you want to add the music to

3 Click on the Insert tab and then click on the arrow below the Sound button on the Media Clips group

4 Click on Play CD Audio Track

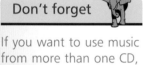

Don't forget

If you want to use music from more than one CD, don't forget to swap the CD before you get to that slide.

Insert CD Audio

Clip selection

Start at track: 1   time: 00:00 seconds

End at track: 1   time: 00:00 seconds

Play options

☐ Loop until stopped

Sound volume:

Display options

☐ Hide sound icon during slide show

Information

Total playing time: 00:00

File: [CD Audio]

OK   Cancel

Hot tip

If you want the music to play continuously, just tick the Loop until stopped button.

5 In the Clip selection area, choose your start and end track

6 Make any other selections you require and then click OK

You will be prompted for how the music will then play. You can choose between Automatically, which will play the music as soon as you go to the slide, or When Clicked, which will only play the music when you click on the CD icon.

Recording sounds

You can record your own sounds or your voice and add it to a slide or slides in the presentation.

1 Select the slide you want to add the sound to

2 Click on the Insert tab and then click on the arrow below the Sound button on the Media Clips group

3 Click on Record Sound and enter a name for the sound

Record Sound	? ✕
Name: Recorded Sound	OK
Total sound length: 0	Cancel
▶ ■ ●	

4 Click the record button to start

5 Click on the stop button when you have finished recording, then click OK to add the sound

The Clip Organizer

The Clip Organizer is a tool that sorts and organizes clips in collections for use in PowerPoint 2007 and other Microsoft Office applications.

You can use it to organize clips that are stored on your machine, or online, and even add and sort new clips.

Using the Clip Organizer

1 From the Microsoft Office Tools program files menu, click on Microsoft Clip Organizer

2 Click the Search button and enter a search

114

3 Or click the Collection List button and look through the available clips in the section that matches your need

4 Click on the clip that you want to use

5 Either press the right mouse button or click on the down arrow that appears to the right of the selected clip

6 Click Copy

7 Go to your presentation and click Paste to insert the clip and move it into position on the slide

Adding Collections and Clips

You can easily add your own collections and clips to the Clip Organizer.

1 Click File and highlight Add Clips to Organizer

2 Choose whether to add the clips automatically (which will search your hard disk and add everything into collections for you) or choose On My Own which gives you the opportunity to select the clips you want to add from any accessible location

3 Choose the clips and click Add to add them

Organizing Clips

Once the clips are in the collections list, you can perform a number of different tasks in order to make it easier to find them later.

These include:

- Renaming, copying or deleting collections
- Copying or moving clips into different collections
- Adding or changing captions on clips
- Changing the properties of a collection
- Adding, modifying or deleting keywords associated with a clip

Hot tip

You can also add clips to your presentation by dragging the clip from the Clip Organizer and dropping it where you want it on the slide.

Hot tip

You can easily add more than one clip at a time by holding down the CTRL key on your keyboard while selecting additional clips.

115

Hot tip

You can even add images from your digital camera or scanner by choosing the Insert Picture from Scanner or Camera option from the Add Clips to Organizer menu.

Photo Albums

If you have ever wanted to create a photo album and deliver it as a presentation, PowerPoint 2007 makes it easy for you.

A Photo Album is a presentation that displays any photographs along with any effects and captions you want to make the presentation more interesting. You can even add frames around the photographs.

Don't forget

You can easily share your photo albums with other people by emailing them or publishing them online.

Creating a Photo Album

1 Click on the Insert tab and click on the arrow under Photo Album from the Illustrations menu

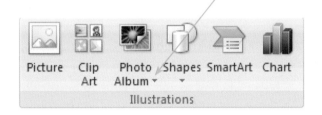

2 Click on New Photo Album to begin the process

Adding Photographs

Hot tip

You can easily add more than one photo at a time by holding down the CTRL key on your keyboard while selecting additional photos.

1 Click on Insert picture from File/Disk button and choose the photographs you want to add

Editing the Album

Once you have added some photographs to the album, you can change the sequence they appear, add captions, add text boxes, and more.

1 Highlight a picture in the album and use the up and down arrows to change the sequence where necessary

Photo Album

Album Content

Insert picture from:

File/Disk...

Insert text:

New Text Box

Picture Options:
☐ Captions below ALL pictures
☐ ALL pictures black and white

Pictures in album:
1   Text Box
2   starbuck.jpg
3   IMG_0861.JPG
4   IMG_0966.JPG
5   IMG_1401.JPG

Preview:

↑ ↓   Remove

Album Layout

Picture layout: Fit to slide

Frame shape: Rectangle

Theme: Browse...

Create   Cancel

Don't forget

Ensure you have the correct codecs installed on your computer in order to play back some of the formats listed.

117

2 Change the picture layout to whatever you want

Changing the Photograph Appearance

1 Select a picture in the album

- To rotate a picture, use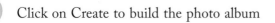

- To change the contrast, use

- To change the brightness, use

2 Click on Create to build the photo album

Media Formats

PowerPoint 2007 supports a number of different audio and video file formats, including:

Audio File Formats

File Format	Description
.aiff	Audio Interchange File Format
.au	UNIX Audio
.mid or .midi	Musical Instrument Digital Inteface
.mp3	MPEG Audio Layer 3
.wav	Wave Form
.wma	Windows Media Audio

Video File Formats

File Format	Description
.asf	Advanced Streaming Format
.avi	Audio Video Interface
.mpg or .mpeg	Moving Picture Experts Group
.wmv	Windows Media Video

QuickTime Movies

Unfortunately you are not able to insert Apple QuickTime movie files (those files with a .mov extension) into your presentation.

If you need to play a QuickTime movie during your presentation, the easiest way of achieving this is to create a hyperlink to the actual .mov file and click on that link during the presentation.

The other option would be to convert the .mov file to one of the supported video file formats. However, this process requires additional software that is not provided as part of the Microsoft Office suite and can sometimes be quite complicated.

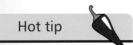

Hot tip

If you want to view your photos in full screen, select Fit to slide from the Picture layout box.

Hot tip

If you want to add captions to a photo you must first specify a layout for the pictures in the album.

Hot tip

To make the presentation look more like a photo album, choose a frame shape after you have chosen the picture layout.

8 Reviewing & Proofing

This chapter will guide you through the process of checking and reviewing your presentation.

Office Language Settings

When you type a word, PowerPoint will identify that word as belonging to a specific language, based on whatever you have set as your keyboard layout.

This language is then used to determine which dictionary to use, how AutoCorrect works, and whatever rules are used to check grammar.

There may be times when you want to use a word or words that belong to a different language. You can tell PowerPoint what language those are.

Hot tip

You can also change the language settings, including the primary editing language, by clicking on Microsoft Office 2007 Language Settings in the Microsoft Office Tools program menu.

1 Highlight the word you want to set the language to

2 Click the Review tab and select the Set Language button

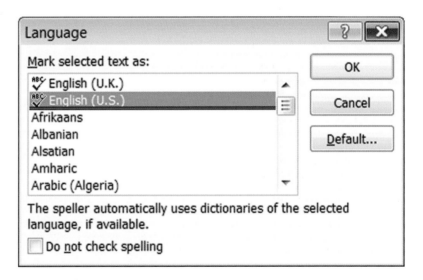

120

Don't forget

Changing the default language will affect the presentation you are working on and all future presentations.

3 Select the language you want to use

4 Click OK

You can also choose not to check the spelling of that word or piece of text by placing a tick in the Do not check spelling box.

Office Proofing Options

To save time and also the need to keep repeating proofing tasks, you can set the defaults on how PowerPoint 2007 will correct and format your presentations.

These include AutoCorrect and spelling, specifically in PowerPoint, both of which will be covered later in this chapter. There are also settings which affect any installed Office programs.

1. Press the Microsoft Office Button and click PowerPoint Options

2. Click Proofing

3. Change any settings you feel the need to change

4. Click Custom Dictionaries to add, remove or create a new dictionary. You can also edit the word list from here

Don't forget

Some of the changes you make in the Proofing options will affect any Office 2007 applications that are installed on your system, not just PowerPoint 2007.

Hot tip

If you have added a lot of words to a dictionary, you can give a copy of it to others for them to use in order to save time and ensure the words are spelt correctly.

121

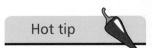

Hot tip

You can buy or download custom dictionaries and add them to PowerPoint to save you from adding lots of new words.

AutoCorrect

AutoCorrect is one of those functions that is just amazing. What it does is to automatically detect and correct any misspelt words or incorrect capitalization. It also aids the quick insertion of symbols, such as the copyright symbol by just typing (c).

 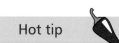
1 Press the Microsoft Office Button and click PowerPoint Options

2 Click Proofing and then click AutoCorrect Options

3 Check or uncheck the relevant options to suit your needs

122

AutoCorrect: English (U.S.)   ? ✕

| AutoCorrect | AutoFormat As You Type | Smart Tags |

☑ Show AutoCorrect Options buttons

☑ Correct TWo INitial CApitals   Exceptions...
☑ Capitalize first letter of sentences
☑ Capitalize first letter of table cells
☑ Capitalize names of days
☑ Correct accidental use of cAPS LOCK key
☑ Replace text as you type

Replace: With:

(c)	©
(r)	®
(tm)	™
...	...
abbout	about

Add   Delete

OK   Cancel

4 You can even add your own words and changes

AutoFormat As You Type

This feature replaces certain types of text entries with something that looks flashier.

If you were to type :-) it would be replaced with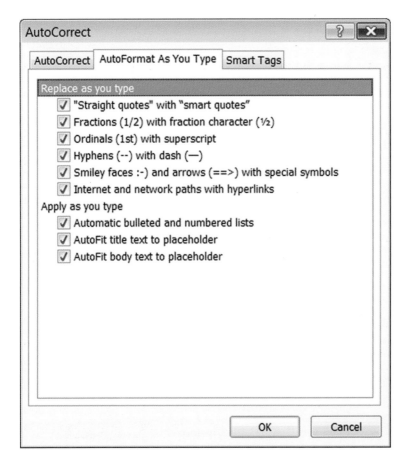

There are also options that are applied as you type, for example, automatic bulleted and numbered lists instead of you having to type the next number in a list, PowerPoint adds it for you.

 Click the AutoFormat As You Type tab

Don't forget

If you don't want your Internet URLs and your network paths shown with hyperlinks automatically, uncheck the Internet and network paths with hyperlinks box.

123

AutoCorrect

| AutoCorrect | AutoFormat As You Type | Smart Tags |

Replace as you type
- ☑ "Straight quotes" with "smart quotes"
- ☑ Fractions (1/2) with fraction character (½)
- ☑ Ordinals (1st) with superscript
- ☑ Hyphens (--) with dash (—)
- ☑ Smiley faces :-) and arrows (==>) with special symbols
- ☑ Internet and network paths with hyperlinks

Apply as you type
- ☑ Automatic bulleted and numbered lists
- ☑ AutoFit title text to placeholder
- ☑ AutoFit body text to placeholder

OK   Cancel

Check or uncheck the relevant options to suit your needs

Spelling

Checking your spelling throughout your presentation is very important. The last thing you want to have done is spent several hours preparing a very important presentation, only to find you have made some spelling mistakes.

Automatic Checking

Some people like to see if they have made a mistake as they are typing. If you are one of these people, then you will want to use the automatic checking capability.

When you type a word that is spelt incorrectly or is not in the dictionary, it is underlined with a red wavy line.

As you can see from the pictur

1 Click the right mouse button over the word, PowerPoint will make suggestions as to what the word might be

2 Click on the word in the list if it appears. If it is the correct spelling, click Add to Dictionary to use again

picture
Ignore All
Add to Dictionary
ABC Spelling...
Cut
Copy
Paste

Enabling or Disabling Automatic checking

To enable or disable automatic checking:

1 Press the Microsoft Office Button

2 Click on PowerPoint Options

3 Select Proofing

Check or uncheck the Check spelling as you type box

Manual Checking

If you are not one of those people who likes to see when they have made a mistake as they make it, or if you find those wavy lines annoying or distracting, you can perform a manual spell check at any time.

Hot tip

You can also start the spelling check at any time by pressing the F7 key.

 Click the Review tab

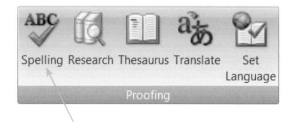

Spelling Research Thesaurus Translate Set Language

Proofing

2 Click the Spelling icon from the Proofing commands menu

Spelling			? ✕
Not in Dictionary:	pictur		
Change to:	picture	Ignore	Ignore All
Suggestions:	picture	Change	Change All
		Add	Suggest
Options...		AutoCorrect	Close

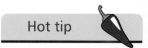

Hot tip

If your have spelt a word incorrectly a number of times, use the Change All button instead of checking each one in turn. The same goes for using the Ignore All button if you don't want to change them.

3 If a word is highlighted and one of the suggestions is correct, highlight that suggestion and click Change

4 You can add the word to your dictionary by clicking Add

5 When you have completed the spelling check, click Close

Researching

Research

Should you need to research a word or topic, PowerPoint 2007 has the ability to search through various reference materials, such as online services, dictionaries and encyclopedia.

1 Click the Review tab and select the Research button from the Proofing commands menu

2 Enter the word or phrase in the Search for: box

3 Select the references or leave on the default All Reference Books

4 Click the Start searching button

You will now be presented with the results, which you can scroll through, depending on the number of hits.

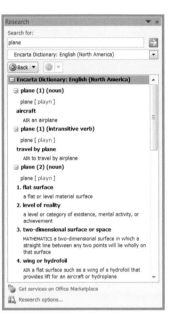

Thesaurus

There is also a thesaurus function which when used, will suggest other words with a similar meaning to the one you select or type.

1 Highlight a word then click the Review tab and select the Thesaurus button from the Proofing commands menu

2 Enter the word or phrase in the entry box

3 Select the references or leave on the default All Reference Books and click the Start searching button in the same way as you did for researching

...cont'd

You can also launch the thesaurus from the presentation.

 Highlight the word you want to check

 Press the right mouse button and highlight Synonyms and choose Thesaurus

no suggestions	Synonyms ▶
Thesaurus...	

Options

There are a number of options you can change relating to both the research functions and the thesaurus, such as the addition or removal of services and also updating existing services.

 Click Research options at the bottom of the Research window

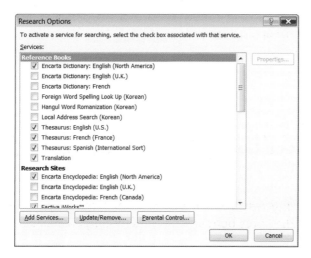

 Check or uncheck the boxes next to the available services as required, or select the Add Services button to add or the Update/Remove button to perform those functions

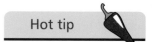

Hot tip

You can add services by selecting them from the advertised services list (if there are any advertised) or by typing the URL of the provider whose services you want to add.

Hot tip

The Parental Control option is there to help control the use of the Research function by utilizing offensive content blocking. Activate this if you want to control what services are used, for example, if you have children who will use PowerPoint. You can even set a password to stop people from changing the settings without your knowledge.

Translation

PowerPoint gives you the ability to translate words or short phrases from one language to another using the Research function.

1 Click the Review tab and select the Translate button from the Proofing commands menu

2 Type the word or phase in the Search for: box

3 Choose the language to translate from and to

4 Click the Start Searching green button to begin

5 Review the translation

Research

Search for:

launch

Translation

Back

Translation

Translate a word or sentence.

From   English (U.S.)

To   French (France)

Translation options...

Bilingual Dictionary

launch

1. lancement *masculin*; chaloupe *féminin*;

2. *verbe transitif* lancer (aussi a ship, a rocket, aussi sens figuré); verbe intransitif: **launch (out) into** se lancer dans

Can't find it?

Try one of these alternatives or see Help for hints on refining your search.

Other places to search

Search for 'launch' in:

All Reference Books

Get services on Office Marketplace

Research options...

Translation Options

These options allow you to choose whether or not to use the online dictionary, and when to use it, and also shows you the available language pairs you can use.

The Bilingual Dictionary is the locally installed dictionary.

1 Click on Translation options

2 Check or uncheck the options as necessary

Comments

By using the Comments features of PowerPoint 2007, you can easily add comments to a slide. These comments can be used for review purposes or as notes to yourself. Each comment has a unique number and initials of the person who left the comment.

Adding a Review Comment

 Click the Review tab and select New Comment from the Comments commands menu

 Type your comment and click anywhere outside of the comment box

> ae2 **andrew edney**   **8/28/2006**
> remember to mention background to this!

 Move the comment box to a specific location on the screen if required

Editing a Review Comment

 Click on the review comment you want to edit

 Click the Edit Comment button

Deleting a Review Comment

 Click on the review comment you want to delete

 Click the Delete button

Hot tip

Use the Next and Previous buttons, on the Comments command menu, to easily step between comments rather than clicking on each individual comment.

Hot tip

To read comments that have been added to the presentation, click the Show Markup button on the comments menu.

Beware

If you are used to using previous versions of PowerPoint, you will notice that the Send for Review option no longer exists. To perform this function now you must email the presentation and reviewers can use the comments feature and then email it back to you.

Outline View

Outline View gives you the ability to just view the text entries on each slide without any backgrounds, graphics or other additions. This can make it very easy to quickly scroll through and check for errors, including spelling mistakes and formatting problems.

1 Select Outline on the PowerPoint window

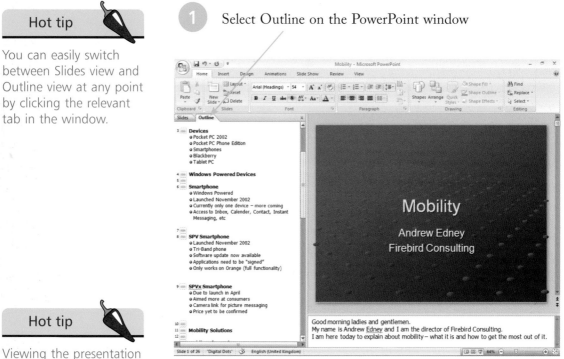

Print Outline View

You can also print the outline view if you find it easier to check the presentation on paper rather than on the screen.

1 Press the Microsoft Office Button

2 Click on Print

3 Select Outline View from the Print what drop-down list

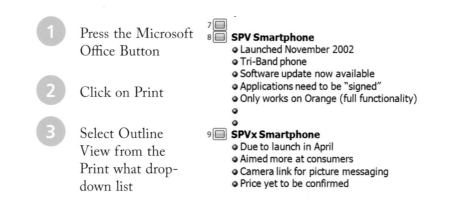

SPV Smartphone
- Launched November 2002
- Tri-Band phone
- Software update now available
- Applications need to be "signed"
- Only works on Orange (full functionality)

SPVx Smartphone
- Due to launch in April
- Aimed more at consumers
- Camera link for picture messaging
- Price yet to be confirmed

9 Creating Slide Shows

This chapter will tell you everything you need to know to create slide shows of your presentations, including adding narration and creating self-running presentations for use in kiosks and demonstrations.

Slide Shows

Once you have finished putting your presentation together, it's time to actually present it, or at the very least, run through it to make sure you are happy with it and see what it will look like from the audiences' perspective.

Starting a Slide Show

1   Click on the Slide Show tab

2   From the Start Slide Show group, select either From Beginning to start from the first slide, or From Current Slide to start from the current point in the presentation

132

3   Run through your presentation or press ESC to end the slide show

Set Up Options

There are a number of options you can change for your slide shows. These include the show type, how you will advance through the slide, what color your default pen will be and even the slide show resolution, among others.

1   Click on the Slide Show tab

2   From the Set Up Slide Show group, select Set Up Slide Show or press the arrow at the bottom-right of the group

Show Type

These options allow you to choose how the presentation will be displayed for your audience.

Show Slides

These options allow you to choose which slides are shown, including the option to specify custom shows.

Don't forget

The list of available pen colors is only available to you if the show type selected is Presented by a speaker (full screen).

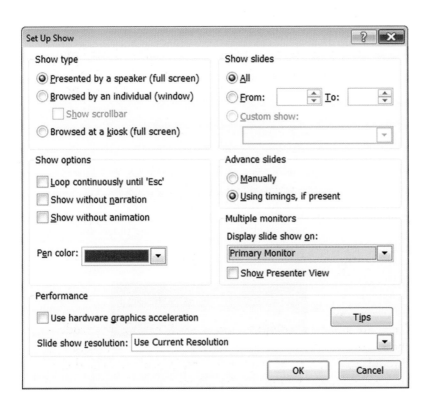

Hot tip

In order to speed up the rendering of graphics in your presentation, check the Use hardware graphics acceleration box, if the graphics card in your computer supports it.

133

Show Options

These options allow you to specify how sounds and animations are run, and you can select the default pen color.

Advance Slides

These options determine how the slides move from one to the next.

Performance

These options are used to specify the level of visual clarity in your presentation.

Beware

Increasing the resolution makes the quality of the presentation better, but there may be a performance hit in doing so.

Rehearsing and Timings

A lot of times when you are presenting, you will have a limited amount of time available to actually deliver the presentation.

You can have PowerPoint 2007 time you while you are rehearsing your presentation so that you know how long you have taken. You can then have PowerPoint 2007 record this time so that you can advance your slides automatically or even use the times to create a self-running presentation.

Don't forget

As soon as you click the Rehearse Timings button the timer begins – so make sure you are ready to present.

1 Click on the Slide Show tab and select Rehearse Timings from the Set Up group

The Rehearsal toolbar enables you to pause the presentation or advance to the next slide.

You can also see the time on current slide and also the total time.

Hot tip

If you want your slides to advance automatically when you present, ensure the Use Rehearsed Timings box is checked. Likewise, if you don't want them to advance, ensure it is unchecked.

2 Work through the rehearsal of your presentation

3 Press ESC to finish the rehearsal and decide if you want to use the newly recorded slide timings when you view your slide show

Microsoft Office PowerPoint

The total time for the slide show was 0:08:50. Do you want to keep the new slide timings to use when you view the slide show?

Yes   No

Writing on Slides

During your slide show, you may want to write on the slides, as though you were using a whiteboard. You can use different types of pens and colors and write anything you want, including underlining, circling or any other freehand writing.

1 At any point during your slide show, when you are on a slide you wish to write on, either press the right mouse button and highlight Pointer Options or at the bottom-left of the screen, click on the pen icon

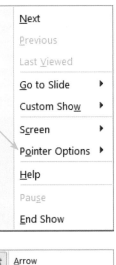

| Next |
| Previous |
| Last Viewed |
| Go to Slide ▸ |
| Custom Show ▸ |
| Screen ▸ |
| Pointer Options ▸ |
| Help |
| Pause |
| End Show |

2 Choose the type of pen you want to use (ballpoint, felt tip or highlighter)

3 Choose the ink color if you want to change it

4 Hold down the left mouse button and drag the chosen pen over the slide to write with

| ▸ Arrow |
| Ballpoint Pen |
| Felt Tip Pen |
| Highlighter |
| Ink Color ▸ |
| Eraser |
| Erase All Ink on Slide |
| Arrow Options ▸ |

135

Scenario Comparison Chart

Device Only	MMIS 2002	Other
Full phone functionality GSM/GPRS/SMS, Includes hands free capabilities	Remote sync of corporate Exchange email, contacts and calendar	Many 3rd party software enhancements
Internet browsing using Pocket IE (supports 128bit SSL)	Optional lightweight browse access to inbox, calendar, contacts, tasks and GAL	Additional security enhancements
Email & IM – Pop, IMAP, Hotmail, MSN Instant Messenger	RSA SecurID dual-authentication	LOB application support
Connectivity - PPTP/RAS to corporation	ISA 2000 firewall integration	
SD Slot for additional memory		

Using Multiple Monitors

You can now deliver a presentation on more than one monitor. For example, you can have your audience view the presentation on one screen, while you view it on another. This other view is known as the Presenter View.

Presenter View

When you use Presenter View, you can run other programs or different views of your presentation without your audience being able to see what you are viewing. You can also:

- See Preview text which shows you what will appear on the screen with your next click

- Use thumbnails of your slides to create a customized presentation as you are presenting

- View your Speaker notes, which are displayed in large clear type to make it easy for you to read

Extending Your Desktop

Before you can use the Presenter View, you have to extend your desktop onto the second monitor.

Don't forget

You will need a computer that has a multiple monitor capability to use these features.

Don't forget

PowerPoint 2007 supports the use of a maximum of two monitors, even if your computer can support more.

1 Press the right mouse button on your Windows Vista desktop and select Personalize

2 Select Display Settings from the list

3 Select 2 for the second monitor

4 Check the Extend the desktop onto this monitor box

5 Set the resolution and colors as appropriate for your second monitor and click OK

Enabling Presenter View

Now that you have enabled multiple monitors in Windows Vista, you can change the presentation resolution, decide which monitor to show the presentation on, and whether or not to enable Presenter View.

1 Click on the Slide Show tab to display the Monitors group

2 Set the resolution or leave as Use Current Resolution

Resolution:	Use Current Resolution ▾
Show Presentation On	▾
☐ Show Presenter View	

Monitors

3 Select the monitor to Show Presentation On

Use Current Resolution ▾

720x480 (Fastest, Lowest Fidelity)
848x480
720x576
800x600
1024x480
1024x768 (Slowest, Highest Fidelity)
Use Current Resolution

4 Check the Show Presenter View box

5 Start the slide show

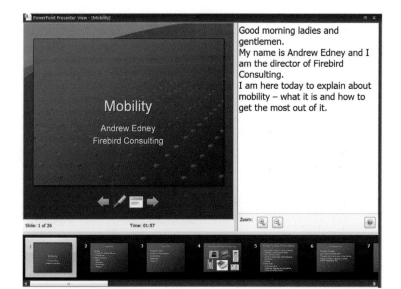

Narration

Narration is a great way to enhance your presentation. It can be used to aid you while you are presenting, or it is best used for self-running presentations, CD packaged presentations, or even for people who could not attend the actual presentation but want to hear what you had to say.

You can record your narration at any time, before your presentation, after your presentation, or even during it should you wish to record any comments or questions from your audience.

Recording a Narration

1 Select the slide you want to begin the narration from

2 Click the Slide Show tab and click on Record Narration from the Set Up group

3 Click on the Set Microphone Level button to check that the recording levels are OK

4 Click OK

5 Should you decide to change the sound quality for any reason (it might not be high enough quality, or it might take up too much disk space) click on the Change Quality button

Sound Selection		
Name:		
[untitled] ▼	Save As...	Remove
Format:	PCM ▼	
Attributes:	11.025 kHz, 8 Bit, Mono 10 kb/sec ▼	
	OK	Cancel

6 You can change the format and the attributes as you see fit – scroll through the attributes to see the quality and the disk space requirements per second of recording, then click OK when you have made your selection

7 Click OK on the Record Narration screen to begin recording

8 After you have finished, decide whether or not to save the slide timings along with the narration

Microsoft Office PowerPoint

ℹ The narrations have been saved with each slide. Do you want to save the slide timings as well?

Save   Don't Save

You will notice that any slide with narration will be shown in the slides window with a star under the slide number.

Slide Transitions

When you change from one slide to the next, this is called a slide transition. You can choose from a large number of different transitions, add sounds, decide how fast the transition is, and much more.

Using the Same Transition for All Slides

1   Click on the Animations tab

2   Click on a slide transition icon from the Transition To This Slide group or click on the More button to see all available transitions

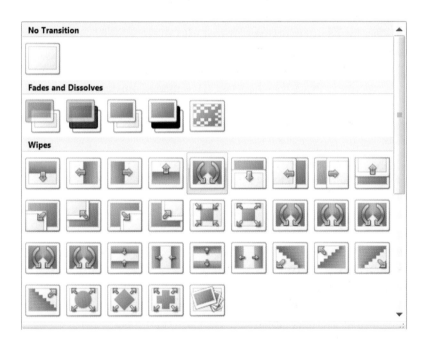

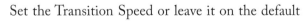

3   Set the Transition Speed or leave it on the default

④ Click on the Apply to All button to set that transition and speed throughout your presentation

Using Different Transitions for Each Slide

① Select the slide you want to transition to

② Click on the Animations tab

③ Click on a slide transition icon from the Transition To This Slide group or click on the More button to see all available transitions

④ Set the Transition Speed or leave it on the default

⑤ Repeat steps 1 – 4 for each slide you want to use a different transition for

Don't forget

If you don't want to use a transition on a slide or slides that you have already set a transition for, choose No Transition from the available transitions menu.

Adding Sounds to Transitions
You can add sounds to the transitions as well.

① Select the slide you want to add the sound to

② Click on the Transition Sound option list and choose a sound or select Other Sound to add your own

 Transition Sound [No Sound] ▾

Advancing Slides
You can choose to have the slide advance on a click of the mouse (which is the default action) or you can set an amount of time before the slide automatically transitions.

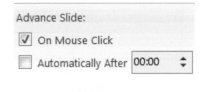

Advance Slide:
☑ On Mouse Click
☐ Automatically After 00:00 ⬍

Custom Slide Shows

You can use a custom slide show to adapt an existing presentation for other audiences without the need to take a complete copy of the presentation and change it, thus having multiple copies.

There are two different types of custom slide shows: basic shows and hyperlinked shows.

Basic Shows

Basic custom shows are separate presentations, or presentations that only contain a subset of slides from your chosen presentation. For example, the presentation to your boss might contain all the slides you have created, but the presentation to your staff may only contain some of them.

Hot tip

Make sure you give your custom shows memorable names to make it easy for you to select the right one. Custom Show 1 may mean something to you when you are creating it, but in a few days time you won't remember what it was!

1 Click on the Slide Show tab

2 Click the arrow on the Custom Slide Show button

3 Click on the Custom Shows button

Custom Shows

Custom shows:

New...

Edit...

Remove

Copy

Close   Show

 4 Click on the New button or select a custom show from the list and click Edit

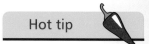

Define Custom Show

Slide show <u>n</u>ame: Custom Show 1

Slides in presentation:

```
12. Slide 12
13. Mobile Information Server 2002
14. Slide 14
15. Slide 15
16. Slide 16
17. Slide 17
18. Slide 18
19. Slide 19
20. Exchange 2003
21. Blackberry
22. Blackberry Enterprise Server
23. Syncrologic Email Accelerator
```

S<u>l</u>ides in custom show:

```
1. Mobility
2. Exchange 2003
3. Slide 18
```

<u>A</u>dd >>   <u>R</u>emove

OK   Cancel

Hot tip

To select multiple slides at the same time, hold down the SHIFT button if the slides are in sequence, or the CTRL button if they are not.

5 Highlight the slides from the presentation and click the Add button to add them to the custom show

6 Use the up and down arrows to change the sequence of the slides in the custom show

7 Give your custom slide show a name and click OK

8 You can then preview your new custom slide show by clicking the Show button

Playing Custom Shows

You can play a custom slide show by selecting it from the list of available custom shows.

To play a custom slide show:

1 Click on the Slide Show tab

2 Click the arrow on the Custom Slide Show button

3 Click on the name of the custom slide show to play it

```
Team 1

Team 2

Team 3

Board

Custom Shows...
```

Hyperlinked Slide Shows

Hyperlinked custom slide shows allow you to navigate to one or more sections within the presentation via a link.

1 Ensure you have created all your custom shows as described in the Basic Shows section

2 Select the text or an object that you want to use as the link

3 Click on the Insert tab, then choose Hyperlinks from the Links group

4 On the Link to list, click on Place in This Document

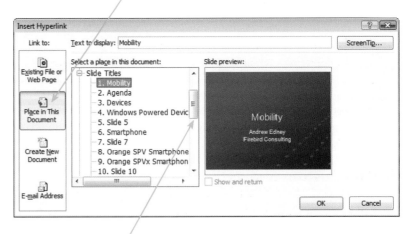

5 Scroll down the Select a place in this document list to Custom Shows

6 Click on the show you want to link to and place a check in the Show and return box then click OK

The text you select to link to will now be underlined. To launch the hyperlink show, just click on the word during the main presentation.

Self-Running Presentations

You may want your presentation to be running without the need for you to be there, for example, in a reception area, at a trade show or in a kiosk.

You can even set the presentation so that other people cannot make changes to it. Effectively you are removing most of the PowerPoint controls from being used.

Self-running presentations will also restart when they have completed their run through and if you have a slide that requires manual input to continue, it will continue automatically after a period of five minutes.

Options

There are a number of options to consider with self-running presentations. These include:

- The use of hyperlinks and actions buttons to guide viewers through the presentation

- Using narration to talk viewers through the presentation as if you were there presenting it to them yourself, as described earlier in this chapter

- The use of timings, so that viewers have enough time to view each slide without feeling rushed or getting bored, also described earlier in this chapter

Kiosk Mode

There is a special option available for slide shows, referred to as Browsed at a kiosk. This enables your presentation to be displayed in full screen and enables the viewer to have additional control over the viewing, if you give them that ability.

1. Click on the Slide Show tab

2. Click the arrow on the Set Up group to launch the Set Up Show dialog box

3. Change the show type to Browsed at a kiosk (full screen) and then click OK

Don't forget

Keep in mind where the self-running presentation will be played. This will help you to determine the best elements to add to your presentation.

Hot tip

You can also package your self-running presentation to run from a CD. See Package for CD in chapter 11.

Don't forget

Make sure to set automatic timings, hyperlinks or action buttons when using kiosk mode or the presentation will get stuck on the first slide.

Keyboard Shortcuts

When you are presenting your slide show, there are a number of keyboard shortcuts that you can use.

Below are a list of some of the more commonly used ones.

Hot tip

Press F1 at any time during a presentation to display the complete list of keyboard shortcuts.

Function	Press
Start a presentation from the beginning	F5
Next animation or go to next slide	N, ENTER
Previous animation or go to previous slide	P, BACKSPACE
Go to slide number...	number+ENTER
Display a black slide or return from one	B
Display a white slide or return from one	W
Stop or restart an automatic presentation	S
End the presentation	ESC
Return to the first slide	1+ENTER
Display the shortcut menu	shift+F10
Perform mouse click on selected hyperlink	ENTER
Go to the first or next hyperlink	TAB
Go to the previous or last hyperlink	SHIFT+TAB
Erase drawing	E
View task bar	CTRL+T

For some functions, there are a number of possible keys that could be used. For example, going to the next slide (as shown above using the N or the ENTER key) can also be achieved using page down, right arrow, down arrow or even the spacebar.

The Slide Sorter

If you want to view your presentation and change the order of the slides easily, you can use the Slide Sorter view.

When you select the Slide Sorter, all of the slides in your presentation are displayed in sequence as thumbnails.

You can then easily drag slides into a new position with the presentation or even delete any of them.

 Click on the Slide Sorter icon near the bottom-right of the screen

Scroll through the slides in the presentation until you come to one you want to move or delete

Click on the slide to highlight it

If you want to move it to a different position, hold the left mouse button down and drag the slide to wherever you want it and release the button

If you want to delete the slide, or add a new slide, press the right mouse button and then click either New Slide or Delete Slide

Click on the Normal icon near the bottom of the screen to return to the normal view

148

Slide Show Options

There are a number of different options that can be set for how PowerPoint performs when using Slide Shows. These options are:

- Show menu on right mouse click – enables or disables the shortcut menu that can be displayed during a slide show, enabling you to select menu options without having to stop the slide show itself

- Show pop-up toolbar – enables or disables the toolbar that appears at the bottom of the screen when displaying a slide show in full screen

- Prompt to keep ink annotations when exiting – enables or disables the prompt to save any annotations that have been made to slides during the slide show

- End with black slide – will display a black slide at the end of the presentation. If this option is not selected when the presentation ends you will be returned to PowerPoint

Hot tip

Enabling the Show menu on right mouse click is very useful if you need to access menu options without stopping the slide show, as it will make the slide show look more professional.

1 Press the Microsoft Office Button and select PowerPoint Options

2 Click on Advanced

3 Scroll down to the section called Slide Show

Hot tip

Always end the slide show with a black screen or other final page rather that just going back into PowerPoint.

Slide Show

☑ Show menu on right mouse click ⓘ
☑ Show popup toolbar ⓘ
☑ Prompt to keep ink annotations when exiting
☑ End with black slide

4 Check or clear the Slide Show options boxes depending on what options you want to enable or disable

5 Click OK to save the changes

10 Saving Your Presentation

This chapter will tell you everything you need to know in order to save in some of the various formats available, including to earlier versions of PowerPoint.

Saving a Presentation

Saving a presentation could not be easier. Now that you have finished your presentation, or have got to a stage where you want to save your progress, you have a number of different options available to you.

Hot tip

You can also initiate the save process by pressing the CTRL + S keys simultanously.

1 Click either the Microsoft Office Button and select Save, or select the floppy disk icon to initiate the save process

2 In the Save In box, select the location where you want your presentation saved

Don't forget

Save your work regularly – this helps ensure that you don't lose anything if your computer experiences a problem.

150

Save As					
« Documents ▸ presentations			▾	✦	Search
Organize ▾ Views ▾ New Folder					
	Name	Date modified	Type	Size	Tags
Favorite Links		This folder is empty.			
Desktop					
Computer					
Recent					
Documents					
Network Shortcuts					
Pictures					
More »					
Folders					

File name: Presentation1

Save as type: PowerPoint Presentation

Authors: andrew edney   Tags: Add a tag

Hide Folders   Tools ▾   Save   Cancel

Hot tip

Use a file name that describes what your presentation is rather than just calling it Presentation1 so that it makes it easier for you to find your file again later.

3 If you need to, create a new folder to save your presentation to

4 In the File name box, enter a name for your presentation

5 Click Save

This will save the presentation in the default .pptx format that is new to PowerPoint 2007.

Choosing a Different Type

By default, when you save a presentation, it is saved as the new PowerPoint 2007 .pptx type.

You can also save as many different types of files.

 1 Perform the same steps as you did to save a presentation only this time do not click Save just yet

2 Click the drop-down arrow on the Save as type box to reveal all the possible file types you can save as

PowerPoint Presentation
PowerPoint Macro-Enabled Presentation
PowerPoint 97-2003 Presentation
PDF
XPS Document
PowerPoint Template
PowerPoint Macro-Enabled Template
PowerPoint 97-2003 Template
Office Theme
PowerPoint Show
PowerPoint Macro-Enabled Show
PowerPoint 97-2003 Show
PowerPoint Add-In
PowerPoint 97-2003 Add-In
PowerPoint XML Presentation
Single File Web Page
Web Page
GIF Graphics Interchange Format
JPEG File Interchange Format
PNG Portable Network Graphics Format
TIFF Tag Image File Format
Device Independent Bitmap
Windows Metafile
Enhanced Windows Metafile
Outline/RTF

Hot tip

Make sure you select the correct type for the presentation you want to save.

3 Select the required file type from the drop-down list

4 Click Save and follow any on screen instructions

Saving as a PDF

PDF is Adobe's Portable Document Format. It is used to share documents and it keeps the format exactly the same as that of the original for ease of viewing and printing. The ability to save a presentation as a PDF is a new feature with PowerPoint 2007 and is very useful when you want to send a presentation to someone to either review or as an electronic handout following a presentation.

Saving as a PDF

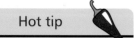

Hot tip

To save or export a file to a PDF or XPS, you may have to install the Publish as PDF or XPS add-in. This add-in is free and can be obtained from the Microsoft Office website if it is not already installed.

1 Follow the same steps as before to save a presentation, only this time select PDF from the Save as type menu or press the Microsoft Office Button and highlight Save As and choose PDF or XPS

Publish as PDF or XPS
« Documents ▸   Search
File name: Presentation1
Save as type: PDF
☐ Open file after publishing   Optimize for: ⦿ Standard (publishing online and printing)
⦾ Minimum size (publishing online)
Options...
⦿ Browse Folders   Tools ▾   Publish   Cancel

Don't forget

In order to view a PDF once you have created it, you must have Adobe Reader installed on your computer. You can download it from http://www.adobe.com if you don't already have it installed.

2 You can have the PDF open automatically once it has been created by selecting the Open file after publishing box

3 Set any optimization you want – Standard (which is the default) is probably sufficient for your purposes as this is the setting for publishing online and printing

4 At this point you can select Publish to complete the process or you can select the Options tab to change or set any additional options you may wish to use

152

Options

For most people, the default option settings will be sufficient. However, if you want to change what is being published, you can do so quite easily.

These settings include:

- Which slides to publish (all, the current slide, or a selection)

- The ability to choose the format and layout (slides, handouts, notes pages or outline views) of what is published

Beware

Any animations, transitions or sound and video will not be preserved when you create the PDF.

Don't forget

The Publish as PDF or XPS add-in works for all Office applications that you have installed on your system, so you don't have to install it for each one.

153

Compatibility Checker

PowerPoint 2007 uses new file formats and contains lots of new features, and not everyone you will want to share your files with will have 2007, there is a risk that part or all of your presentation may not be compatible with earlier versions of PowerPoint.

This is where the Compatibility Checker comes in to play.

When you select Compatibility Checker or save a presentation in a down-level format (PowerPoint 97–2003), and your presentation contains some of the new features, you will be presented with the Compatibility Checker.

The results of the compatibility checker will display:

- Any incompatibilities in the presentation

- What the behavior will be when viewed in earlier versions

- How many occurrences of each specific type exist

1 Press the Microsoft Office Button and highlight Prepare

2 Select Run Compatibility Checker

	Run Compatibility Checker
	Check for features not supported by earlier versions of PowerPoint.

Don't forget

Always read what is displayed in the Compatibility Checker summary as you don't want people not to be able to view your presentations!

Microsoft Office PowerPoint Compatibility Checker

Because some of the features in this presentation are not supported by versions of PowerPoint earlier than PowerPoint 2007, the features will be lost or degraded if saved in this format. Click Continue to save the presentation anyway.

Summary	Number of occurrences
The effects applied to the text will be slightly modified, but the text will remain editable.	22
The text, graphic, and the applied effects will be combined as one object, making it un-editable.	1

☑ Check compatibility when saving this presentation.

Continue   Cancel

New Formats

You may have noticed if you have already saved a presentation, or tried to open a presentation, that PowerPoint 2007 uses a different file format called PowerPoint XML (.pptx).

This new format saves presentations as much smaller files than .ppt's used to and there is also improved recovery of corrupt or damaged files.

There are a number of new XML file types supported by PowerPoint 2007, along with a number of existing file types.

New file types and extensions

The following table highlights the new XML file types and their extensions.

Extension	XML File Type
.pptx	PowerPoint Presentation
.pptm	Macro-enabled presentation
.potx	Template
.potm	Macro-enabled template
.ppam	Macro-enabled add-in
.ppsx	Show
.ppsm	Macro-enabled show
.sldx	Slide
.sldm	Macro-enabled slide
.thmx	Office theme
.pdf	PDF file
.xps	XPS document
.pps	Show

Don't forget

Users of earlier versions of PowerPoint will not be able to open these new file types.

Default Saving Options

You can tell PowerPoint the format of the files that you save as a default, including setting the time for autosaves and default file locations.

The format choices are either PowerPoint Presentation which is the new PowerPoint 2007 format, PowerPoint Macro-Enable Presentation or PowerPoint Presentation 97–2003.

156

1 Press the Microsoft Office Button and select PowerPoint Options

2 Click Save from the left-hand column

Customize how documents are saved.

Preserve backup information for your presentations

Save files in this _format:_ PowerPoint Presentation

☑ Save _AutoRecover_ information every 10 ⬆⬇ minutes

Default _file_ location: C:\Users\andrew edney\Documents\

Offline editing options for document management server files

Save checked-out files to: ⓘ
 ⦿ The server drafts _location_ on this computer
 ◯ The _web_ server

Server drafts location: C:\Users\andrew edney\Documents\SharePoint Drafts\   Browse...

Preserve fidelity when sharing this presentation: 📄 Presentation1 ▾

☐ _Embed_ fonts in the file ⓘ
 ⦿ Embed _only_ the characters used in the presentation (best for reducing file size)
 ◯ Embed all _characters_ (best for editing by other people)

3 Choose the format to save files

| PowerPoint Presentation |
| PowerPoint Macro-Enabled Presentation |
| PowerPoint Presentation 97-2003 |

4 Set the time for saving autorecover information

5 Change the default file location if necessary

Saving for the Web

You can save your presentation directly to a web server formatted for publication on the Internet.

1 Press the Microsoft Office Button and select Save As

2 Choose Web Page from the Save as type drop-down box

3 Click Change Title to add a title that will appear in the title bar of the browser

4 Click the Publish button to display the Publish as Web Page options

5 Change any options as necessary, including adding the location of where you want to publish the slides to

6 Click the Publish button

Hot tip

Publishing to a website is very useful if you want a large number of people to see your presentation but you don't want to provide it as a PowerPoint file.

Hot tip

Each slide will be created as a separate HTML file so you can link to any file or reuse any file on your website if you wish.

Don't forget

If you are planning on publishing directly to a web server, make sure the server is available and that you have the correct permissions to publish on that server.

Saving in an Earlier Format

If you want to save your presentation in an earlier PowerPoint format in order to share with someone who does not have PowerPoint 2007, it is very easy to do.

Don't forget
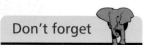

If you have used any of the new features of PowerPoint 2007 in your presentation, they may not be available in the 97–2003 presentation.

1 Press the Microsoft Office Button and highlight Save As

2 Select PowerPoint 97–2003 Presentation

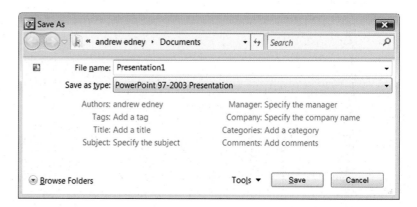

158

Beware

PowerPoint 97–2003 does not recognize the new SmartArt graphics and visual objects of 2007. These will automatically be converted to bitmaps to maintain their appearance.

3 In the Save In box, select the location where you want your presentation saved

4 In the File name box, enter a name for your presentation

5 Click Save

Compatibility with Earlier Versions of PowerPoint

Users of PowerPoint 2000, XP or 2003 can download a file format converter patch from Microsoft Office Online which will give them the ability to open, edit and save files using the new XML format. The minimum installed service pack to use the converter is as follows:

Don't forget

You must download and install the patch before you can use the new formats.

- Office 2000 Service Pack 3

- Office XP Service Pack 3

- Office 2003 Service Pack 1

11 Sharing Presentations

This chapter will guide you through the process of preparing your presentation for sharing with others. This includes checking for personal information in the presentation to printing and publishing and even writing it to CD.

Presentation Properties

Each document has a number of properties associated with it. These properties are often referred to as metadata and include:

- Presentation title

- Author information

- Keywords

Properties

 Press the Microsoft Office Button, choose Prepare and select Properties

Properties
View and edit presentation properties, such as Title, Author, and Keywords.

Hot tip

By entering values in the various properties boxes you can organize presentations and make it easier later to find what you are searching for by using that metadata.

This brings up the standard properties box. As you can see, some of the fields are populated by default, such as author name

Properties: Standard ▼				* = Required field ✕
Author:	Title:	Subject:	Keywords:	
Andrew Edney	Slide 1			
Category:	Status:			
Comments:				

Standard properties enable you to enter metadata for:

- Author
- Subject
- Category
- Comments
- Title
- Keywords
- Status

Enter any information you want in these boxes. The keywords field is particularly useful

...cont'd

Advanced Properties

Choosing the advanced properties option gives you a greater level of control over what you can add or change.

 1 Click on Document Properties to bring up the advanced options

> ⓘ Document Properties ▼
>   🖅 Advanced Properties...

Advanced properties gives you additional information, including:

- What template is being used
- Various statistics on the presentation
- Document contents and custom fields

2 Navigate the tabs and enter any information you want

3 Click OK to finish

Don't forget

The more metadata you add to your presentation, the easier it may be later to search for something specific.

161

Hot tip

Custom fields can be very useful if you need to add specific metadata to your presentation that is not already defined. Metadata that can be added include text, time, numerical values or even yes or no.

Inspecting Documents

As you are planning on sharing your presentation, it would be a good idea to check that there is no personal information or hidden data within it. This hidden data could contain information about you or your organization that you don't want to share.

Document Inspector

 Press the Microsoft Office Button, choose Prepare and select Inspect Document to launch the Document Inspector

> **Inspect Document...**
> Check the presentation for hidden metadata or personal information.

2 Choose the types of content that you want to inspect by placing a check in the box for each one

---

Document Inspector

To check the document for the selected content, click Inspect.

☑ **Comments and Annotations**
Inspects the document for comments and ink annotations.

☑ **Document Properties and Personal Information**
Inspects for hidden metadata or personal information saved with the document.

☑ **Custom XML Data**
Inspects for custom XML data stored with this document.

☑ **Invisible On-Slide Content**
Inspects the presentation for objects that are not visible because they have been formatted as invisible. This does not include objects that are covered by other objects.

☐ **Off-Slide content**
Inspects the presentation for objects that are not visible because they are outside the slide area. This does not include objects with animation effects.

☑ **Presentation Notes**
Inspects the presentation for information in the presenter's notes.

Inspect   Close

Click Inspect to begin the inspection process

> **Document Inspector**
>
> Currently running Inspector 4 of 6:
> Invisible On-Slide Content
>
> Cancel

Hot tip

Always use a copy of your presentation so that anything that is removed is still available to you in the original. You may still need it!

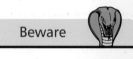

④ Check the results carefully and click the Remove All button against whichever type of hidden content you want to remove

> **Document Inspector**
>
> Review the inspection results.
>
> ✓ **Comments and Annotations**
> No items were found.
>
> ❗ **Document Properties and Personal Information**   [Remove All]
> The following document information was found:
> * Document properties
>
> ✓ **Custom XML Data**
> No custom XML data was found.
>
> ✓ **Invisible On-Slide Content**
> No invisible objects found.
>
> ✓ **Presentation Notes**
> No presentation notes were found.
>
> ⚠ Note: Some changes cannot be undone.
>
> [Reinspect]   [Close]

Beware

Some changes cannot be undone so it is advisable to save your presentation before making any changes you are unsure of.

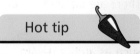

⑤ You can then choose to recheck the document by clicking the Reinspect button

Hot tip

Document Inspector also works on presentations created in versions of PowerPoint prior to PowerPoint 2007.

⑥ Click Close to finish the inspection process

Marking as Final

The Mark As Final option in PowerPoint 2007 is used to make the presentation read-only and prevent changes from being made once you have shared it.

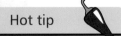

Hot tip

Use Mark As Final to communicate to the people you are sharing the presentation with that it is complete.

Mark As Final

1 Press the Microsoft Office Button, choose Prepare and select Mark As Final

> **Mark As Final**
> Let readers know the presentation is final and make it read-only.

Beware

Even though you have marked the presentation as final, anyone can remove the Mark As Final status from the presentation and edit it.

164

> **Microsoft Office PowerPoint** ✕
>
> ⚠ This presentation will be marked as final and then saved.
>
> OK   Cancel

2 Click OK to mark the presentation as final and save it. The process for saving a presentation should be followed as normal

Unmarking As Final

If you need to edit the presentation or add to it, you will need to run through the same process again, only this time it unmarks it as final.

Beware

Presentations marked as final in PowerPoint 2007 will not be read-only when opened in earlier versions of PowerPoint.

1 Press the Microsoft Office Button, choose Prepare and select Mark As Final again

2 Continue working on the presentation

3 When you are ready to Mark As Final again, run through the steps listed above

Package for CD

One of the easiest ways to share your presentation with others is on CD. When you use the Package for CD functionality in PowerPoint 2007, you also have a number of options including the ability to make the presentation or presentations self-running packages without the need for users to have PowerPoint.

Package for CD

 Press the Microsoft Office Button, choose Publish and select Package for CD

> **Pac_kage for CD**
> Copy the presentation and media links to a folder that can be burned to a CD.

2 Enter a name for the CD and click Add Files to add additional presentations to be written

Package for CD

Copy presentations to a CD that will play on computers running Microsoft Windows 2000 or later, even without PowerPoint.

Name the CD: | PresentationCD

Play order | Files to be copied
1 | Mobility.pptx
2 | Options.pptx
3 | Business Plan.pptx

[Add...]
[Remove]

Linked files and the PowerPoint Viewer are included by default. To change this, click Options.

[Options...]

[Copy to Folder...]   [Copy to CD]   [Close]

3 Click Options to set the various additional options available

...cont'd

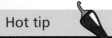
Hot tip

If you want to make your CD presentations look slicker, you can set them to play automatically when a user inserts the CD and have them play in the specified order if that is important to the content.

Don't forget

It's always a good idea to inspect the presentations for personal information or hidden data before sharing them.

Beware

Linked files can be used by hackers to introduce elements to your presentations that you do not want to have.

4 Here you can change the package type, whether to include linked files, set passwords and even inspect the presentation prior to writing it to CD

Options ? ✕

Package type

◉ Make a self-running package

    Select how presentations will play in the viewer:

    | Play all presentations automatically in the specified order | ▼ |

○ Make a package by using original file formats

Include these files

(These files will not display in the Files to be copied list)

☑ Linked files

☐ Embedded TrueType fonts

Security and privacy

Password to open each file: [   ]

Password to modify each file: [   ]

☐ Inspect presentations for inappropriate or private information

            [OK]   [Cancel]

| Play all presentations automatically in the specified order |
| Play only the first presentation automatically |
| Let the user select which presentation to view |
| Don't play the CD automatically |

---

5 After you have made your required changes, click OK

6 Click Copy to CD to begin writing the CD

7 After the CD has finished writing, you have the option to write another CD with the same files

Viewing from CD

When you have a CD that contains a packaged set of PowerPoint files, all you need to do to view them is put the CD in the drive.

1 Put the CD in the CD drive

2 Accept the terms for the PowerPoint Viewer if presented with them

3 Choose the presentation to view if presented with that option (this will only appear if the CD was written with the Let the user select which presentation to view option) otherwise the presentation will play automatically

Don't forget

You don't need to have PowerPoint installed on the computer you wish to view the presentation on if the CD was written with the make a self-running package option, as a PowerPoint viewer is included on the CD automatically.

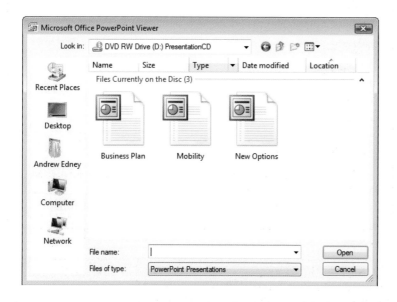

4 Enter the password to open the file if prompted

Printing your Presentation

Printing a presentation is very easy, all you have to do is decide what, how and where you want to print.

Make sure you have selected the printer you want to print to, and that it is switched on, and has paper in it.

168

Hot tip

Its always a good idea to tick the Scale to fit paper box to print better slides.

1 Press the Microsoft Office Button and choose Print

2 Select whether you want to print all slides, the current slide, or a selection of the slides

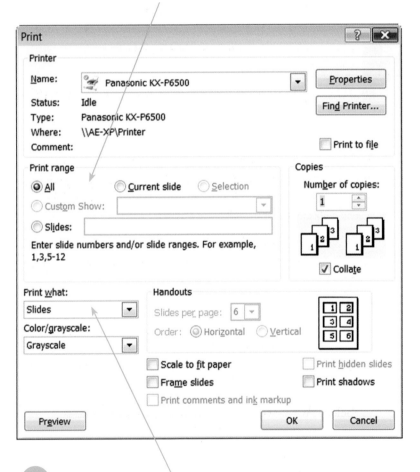

Hot tip

Use the Quick Print option from the Print menu to print the presentation directly to the default printer without making any changes.

3 Select what you want to print

4 Select any other options

5 Click OK to begin printing

Print Options

PowerPoint gives you the ability to print four different types of output from your presentation. You can choose from these four types from the Print what drop-down box.

Slides
This option prints the slides exactly as they are on screen, depending on what other options may have been chosen.

Handouts
Handouts are prints of the slides designed specifically to give to people to take away from the presentation. You can print one slide per page, or a maximum of nine slides per page.

Notes pages
This option will print any of the speakers notes (if there are any) along with each slide.

Outline View
This option prints only the text from each slide – any graphics are not printed. This option can be very useful if you want to quickly and easily see what text is within the slides without having to go through all the slides in depth.

PowerPoint Printing Options
You can set the way PowerPoint prints your presentations from the Print settings within PowerPoint Options.

1 Click the Microsoft Office Button and select PowerPoint Options

2 Select Advanced

3 Check or clear the options you want to set

4 Click OK

Hot tip

When you choose to print 3 slides per page in Handouts mode, a number of blank lines are placed to the right of each slide for note taking purposes.

Don't forget

If you choose to print in color but you don't have a color printer, the prints will print out in similar quality to grayscale.

169

Beware

If you select Pure Black and White from the print options, certain features may not print as the presentation will be printed using only black and white not grayscale.

Print

- ☑ Print in background
- ☐ Print TrueType fonts as graphics
- ☐ Print inserted objects at printer resolution
- ☐ High quality
- ☐ Align transparent graphics at printer resolution

When printing this document: 📑 Mobility ▼

- ○ Use the most recently used print settings ⓘ
- ◉ Use the following print settings: ⓘ

  Print what: Slides ▼

  Color/grayscale: Color ▼

  - ☐ Print hidden slides
  - ☐ Scale to fit paper
  - ☐ Frame slides

Previewing

You can preview what you are about to print by using the Print Preview option.

 1 Press the Microsoft Office Button and hover over the Print arrow

2 Select Print Preview from the available options

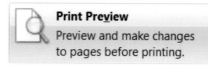

Print Preview
Preview and make changes
to pages before printing.

You can do pretty much anything print wise from the print preview menu. Use this instead of the other print menus to save yourself some time and paper.

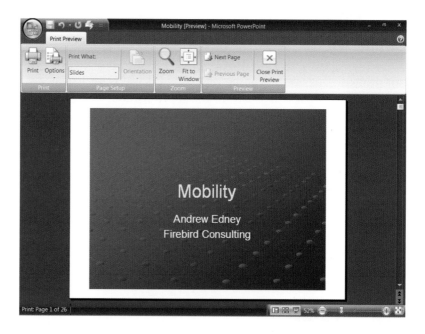

3 From here you can perform many functions, including viewing the slides of the presentation you want to print, change print options, choose what to print, zoom in on slides

4 Press Print to start printing or choose Close Print Preview

Printer Properties

Before you actually start printing, it is a good idea to make sure that you have configured your printer exactly how you want it.

1 Press the Microsoft Office Button and choose Print

2 Select the printer you want to use and click Properties

3 Properties you can change could include page order, paper type, print quality and so on

Don't forget

Different printers have different properties that you can change. If in doubt about the printer's capabilities consult the manual that came with your printer.

171

Panasonic KX-P6500 Document Properties

Layout | Paper/Quality

Orientation:
Ⓐ Landscape

Page Order:
Front to Back

Page Format

Pages per Sheet   1

☐ Draw Borders

Advanced...

OK   Cancel

Panasonic KX-P6500 Advanced Options

Panasonic KX-P6500 Advanced Document Settings
- 📄 Paper/Output
  - Paper Size: A4
  - Copy Count: 1 Copy
- 📊 Graphic
  - Print Quality: 300 x 300 dots per inch
- 📑 Document Options
  - Advanced Printing Features: Enabled
  - Pages per Sheet Layout: Right then Down
  - Halftoning: Auto Select
  - Print Optimizations: Enabled

OK   Cancel

Publishing

You can publish any or all of your slides to a slide library or any other location by using the Publish Slides option in PowerPoint.

1 Press the Microsoft Office Button, highlight Publish and select Publish Slides from the available options

Publish Slides...
Save slides to a Slide Library
or other location to reuse later.

2 Tick the box or boxes for the slides you want to publish

Publish Slides

Select slides that you want to publish.

Thumbnail	File Name	Description
✓	Mobility_001	Mobility
✓	Mobility_002	Agenda
☐	Mobility_016	Devices
☐	Mobility_017	Windows Powered Devices
☐	Mobility_015	

Select All   Clear All   ☐ Show Only Selected Slides

Publish To: [▼] Browse...

Publish   Cancel

3 Enter the location of where you want to publish and click Publish

 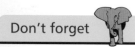

Document Management

You can also publish your presentation to a document management server, such as Microsoft SharePoint Server. Once the presentation has been published all the features of a document management server can be used, such as Check In and Check Out of the presentation, view different versions and even using Workflow.

Don't forget

The sorts of features that will be available to you, once you have published your presentation, will be dependent on the document management server.

 Press the Microsoft Office Button, highlight Publish and select Document Management Server

 Document Management Server
Share the presentation by saving it to a document management server.

 Enter the location of where you want to publish the slides and click Save

Creating a Document Workspace

A Document Workspace is a Microsoft SharePoint website, which can be used to publish your presentations and use features such as Workflow.

Don't forget

To utilize the collaboration and workflow functionality you will need access to Microsoft Office SharePoint Server 2007, Windows SharePoint Services or Microsoft Office Groove 2007.

 Press the Microsoft Office Button, highlight Publish and select Create Document Workspace

 Type in a name for the new Document Workspace

 Type in the URL of your SharePoint server or select it from the drop-down list

 Click Create to complete the process

Document Management ▼ ✕

Document Workspace

Create a Document Workspace site if you want to share a copy of this document with others. Your local copy of the document will be synchronized with the server so that you can see your changes and work on the document with others. When you click Create, a new site is created automatically.

ⓦ Tell me more...

Document Workspace name:

Untitled

Location for new workspace:

(Type new URL) ▼

Create

Hot tip

Using Workflow is a great way to manage the review process of your presentation. You can see the different stages of the process and know the current position.

Word Handouts

You can also create handouts in Microsoft Office Word. These are very useful if you want to share your presentation with others and have them either add comments to it or for them to copy sections into other documents.

1 Press the Microsoft Office Button, highlight Publish and select Create Handouts in Microsoft Office Word

> **Create Handouts in Microsoft Office Word**
> Open the presentation in Word and prepare custom handout pages.

You can then choose the desired page layout including Notes next to slides or Outline only. Also whether or not to add the slides or the actual Word document as well or whether to include a link.

Send To Microsoft Office Word

Page layout in Microsoft Office Word

○ Notes next to slides

○ Blank lines next to slides

○ Notes below slides

○ Blank lines below slides

○ Outline only

Add slides to Microsoft Office Word document

● Paste

○ Paste link

OK   Cancel

2 Select the desired page layout

3 Select whether to paste the slides or to paste a link to the slides then click OK

174

A Microsoft Office Word document is then created from your presentation using the parameters you selected. You can then email the Word document to anyone or place it on a website.

Slide 1

Mobility

Andrew Edney
Firebird Consulting

Good morning ladies and gentlemen. My name is Andrew Edney and I am the director of Firebird Consulting.
I am here today to explain about mobility – what it is and how to get the most out of it.

12 Security

This chapter will guide you through some of the features that help you make your use of PowerPoint, and your presentations, more secure.

Using Passwords

If you want to stop others from modifying your presentation, or even opening it, you can set a password to protect it. Each time that the file is then attempted to be opened or modified (depending on what has been configured) a password must be entered.

Setting a Password

To set a password, make sure the presentation you want to protect is open. Click on the Microsoft Office Button and Select Save As.

1 Click on the Tools button

Tools ▼

Map Network Drive...

2 Select General Options

Save Options...

General Options...

Web Options...

Compress Pictures...

General Options   ? ✖

General Options

File encryption settings for this document

Password to <u>o</u>pen:

File sharing settings for this document

Password to <u>m</u>odify:

Privacy options

☐ <u>R</u>emove automatically created personal information from this file on save

Macro security

Adjust the security level for opening files that might contain macro viruses, and specify the names of trusted macro developers.

Macro <u>S</u>ecurity...

OK   Cancel

3 Enter a password to be used to either open the presentation or modify the presentation (or both)

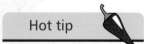

4 Check or clear the Remove automatically created personal information from this file on save box

5 Click OK to continue

6 You will then be prompted to confirm the password you just typed

Confirm Password

Reenter password to open:

●●●●●●●●●|

Caution: If you lose or forget the password, it cannot be recovered. It is advisable to keep a list of passwords and their corresponding document names in a safe place. (Remember that passwords are case-sensitive.)

OK   Cancel

7 Click OK to finish

Using a Password Protected Presentation

Now that you have a password protected presentation, you will be asked to enter the password when you want to open it, modify it, or both (depending on what you selected previously).

1 Enter the password when prompted to open the file

Password

Enter password to open file mypresentation

●●●●●●●●●|

OK   Cancel

Don't forget

Automatically created personal information includes such information as author, title, notes, XML information and more, and so you may not actually want that to be shared with others.

Beware

If you set a password to stop someone from modifying your presentation, there is nothing to stop them from just copying the content into another presentation that they can modify!

177

Don't forget

Whatever you do, don't forget the password. If you do, you will not be able to open or edit the presentation again. If you write it down, make sure it is somewhere safe but not obvious to anyone looking for it.

Restricting Permissions

You can also restrict people's ability to edit, copy or print the presentation, using the Restrict Permission options.

Setting Permissions

1 Press the Microsoft Office Button, then highlight Prepare followed by Restrict Permission

Restrict Permission
Grant people access while restricting their ability to edit, copy, and print.

✓ Unrestricted Access
Restricted Access
Manage Credentials

2 Choose to either leave the default Unrestricted Access selected, or select Restricted Access to specify a list of users and their permissions, or Manage Credentials to change the log-in credentials

3 Follow the steps to sign up for a free trial to the Microsoft Information Rights Management Service

4 Select Manage Credentials to this presentation box and enter email addresses in the Read and Change boxes as required

Permission

☑ Restrict permission to this presentation

Enter the e-mail addresses of users in the Read and Change boxes (example: 'someone@example.com'). Separate names with a semicolon(;). To select names from the Address book, click the Read or Change button.

Read...
Users with Read permission can read this presentation, but cannot change, print or copy content.

Change...
Users with Change permission can read, edit and save changes to this presentation, but cannot print content.

More Options...

OK   Cancel

5 Click on More Options to specify additional permissions

Available Permissions

Apart from changing a user's access level, additional permissions are available to be set, including:

- This presentation expires on: you can set a date when the presentation expires

- Print content: allows the presentation to be printed

In addition, you can add an email address where users can request additional permissions.

Don't forget

Make sure that you choose the permissions you want to use very carefully.

Permission

☑ Restrict permission to this presentation

The following users have permission to this presentation:

Name	Access Level
⬛⬛⬛@hotmail.com	Full Control

Add...
Remove

Additional permissions for users:

☐ This presentation expires on:

Enter date in format: dd/MM/yyyy

☐ Print content
☐ Allow users with read access to copy content
☐ Access content programmatically

Additional settings:

☑ Users can request additional permissions from:

mailto:⬛⬛⬛@hotmail.com

☐ Require a connection to verify a user's permission

Set Defaults...

OK   Cancel

179

Beware

Users may still be able to circumvent some of these permissions using other software or even just by copying the information by hand.

① Change any permissions as required then click OK

A presentation that has restricted permissions will display a Do Not Distribute bar at the top of the screen. Click on the Change Permissions button if you need to change any permissions.

ⓘ **Restricted Access** Permission is currently restricted. Only specified users can access this content.   Change Permission...

Digital Signatures and IDs

PowerPoint gives you the ability to sign a presentation with a digital signature, also known as a digital ID. A digital signature is like your "real" signature only is invisible and is used to ensure the integrity of your presentation by assuring that the content has not been altered since you signed it.

Getting a Digital ID

If you don't already have a digital ID, you will need to either buy one or create one, depending on what you want to use it for.

1 Choose Add a Digital Signature by pressing the Microsoft Office Button and highlighting Prepare

> **Add a Digital Signature**
> Ensure the integrity of the presentation by adding an invisible digital signature.

Hot tip

If you want to sign presentations that will be shared with people for business reasons, you might want to consider obtaining an ID from a Microsoft partner as it can be verified easily.

2 Select OK and then you will be presented with the choice to either Get a digital ID from a Microsoft partner or Create your own digital ID. If you choose to get one from a Microsoft partner, you will be presented with a list of companies who can supply you with one. For now, select Create your own digital ID

Get a Digital ID

In order to sign a Microsoft Office document, you need a digital ID. You have two options for getting a digital ID:

◉ **Get a digital ID from a Microsoft partner**
If you use a digital ID from a Microsoft partner, other people will be able to verify the authenticity of your signature.

○ **Create your own digital ID**
If you create your own digital ID, other people will not be able to verify the authenticity of your signature. You will be able to verify the authenticity of your signature, but only on this computer.

Learn more about digital IDs in Office...   OK   Cancel

Create a Digital ID

Enter the information to be included in your digital ID.

Name: Andrew Edney
E-mail address:
Organization:
Location:

Create   Cancel

3 Enter your details to create your digital ID. These must include your name, email address, organization (if applicable) and location. Then click on the Create button to finish

Signing a Presentation

Now that you have your digital ID, you can sign your presentation.

 Add a comment into the Purpose for signing this document box. Then click Sign to finish

Viewing a Signature

You can view a signature on any signed presentation.

 Choose View Signatures by pressing the Microsoft Office Button and highlighting Prepare

View Signatures
Verify the integrity of the presentation and see who has signed it.

 Click on any valid signature and use the drop-down list to either view the signature details or remove the signature if it is your signature

Signatures ▼ ✕

Valid signatures:

Andrew Edney 1/8/2007

This document is signed.
Any edits made to this document will invalidate the digital signatures.

Learn more about signatures in Office documents...

The Trust Center

The Trust Center is where the security and privacy settings for all Microsoft Office programs are managed.

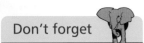
Because the Trust Center controls the security and privacy settings for all Microsoft Office programs, settings you make here may affect other programs and not just PowerPoint.

1 To access the Trust Center, click the Microsoft Office Button, followed by PowerPoint Options and then Trust Center

Beware

If you are not sure what a setting does or the effect it might have on your system, do not enable it. Take a look at the help files relevant to the setting to gain a better understanding.

2 Then just click on the Trust Center Settings button

Add-ins

Add-ins are features that can enhance PowerPoint. These features could include templates, smart-tags and other useful additions. Here is where you can require that Add-ins are signed or even disable all Add-ins.

Message Bar

The Message Bar is very useful for warning you about content that PowerPoint has blocked. The Message Bar will appear under the Ribbon if a problem or potential problem arises. You can change the setting here if you do not want to see information about blocked content.

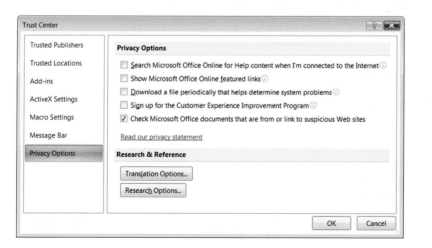

Privacy Options

This is a useful set of options. Here you can enable or disable various privacy options including allowing the searching of Microsoft Office Online for Help content and even checking Microsoft Office documents that are from or link to suspicious websites. This option is very useful as it can be used to help protect you from potential phishing attacks.

183

Beware

Always ensure that the Show the Message Bar in all applications when content has been blocked is enabled, as it is a very good idea to know if you might have a security problem.

Don't forget

Some of the Privacy Options allow either downloads from Microsoft or even uploading of information to Microsoft. Make sure you are happy to allow this before enabling those options.

Hot tip

It is a good idea to enable the Search Microsoft Office Online for Help content option, as this will give you access to up to date help documentation.

Macros

A macro is a piece of code that is used to automate frequently performed tasks.

Macros can contain code that you don't want to run on your computer, such as deleting all your files, or introducing a virus, so always take care when running them.

Before enabling a macro, the Trust Center will perform a number of checks, including the following:

- The macro is signed by the developer with a digital signature

- The digital signature is valid

- The digital signature has not expired

- The certificate that is associated with the digital signature has been issued by a reputable Certificate Authority (CA)

- The developer who signed the macro is a trusted publisher

If any problems are detected, the macro is automatically disabled and you are notified of a potentially unsafe macro, and also given the option of enabling it if you are sure of what it will do and where it has come from.

🛡 **Security Warning**   Macros have been disabled. | Options... |

Microsoft Office Security Options

🛡 **Security Alert - Macro**

Macro

Macros have been disabled. Macros might contain viruses or other security hazards. Do not enable this content unless you trust the source of this file.

Warning: It is not possible to determine that this content came from a trustworthy source. You should leave this content disabled unless the content provides critical functionality and you trust its source.

More information

File Path: C:\Users\Andrew Edney\Desktop\pp machine\dodgy.ppt

- ● Help protect me from unknown content (recommended)
- ○ Enable this content

Open the Trust Center | OK | | Cancel |

Macros Settings

There are four macro settings to choose from. They are:

- Disable all macros without notification – all macros will be disabled and you will not be advised when this happens

- Disable all macros with notification – this is the default, and you will be advised when this happens so that you can choose to allow a macro if you are sure

- Disable all macros except digitally signed macros – any macros digitally signed by a trusted publisher will run, and all others will be disabled

- Enable all macros – this setting allows all macros to run

Changing Macro Settings

You can change the settings that the Trust Center uses when detecting macros by first accessing the Trust Center.

 Choose Macro Settings from the Trust Center menu

185

Trust Center

Trusted Publishers
Trusted Locations
Add-ins
ActiveX Settings
Macro Settings
Message Bar
Privacy Options

Macro Settings

For macros in documents not in a trusted location:
- ○ Disable all macros without notification
- ● Disable all macros with notification
- ○ Disable all macros except digitally signed macros
- ○ Enable all macros (not recommended, potentially dangerous code can run)

Developer Macro Settings

☐ Trust access to the VBA project object model

OK   Cancel

2 Select the setting that you want to use

3 Check Trust access to the VBA project object model only if you are the developer and want to enable this trust

4 Click OK

ActiveX

ActiveX controls are components that can be anything from a simple box to a toolbar or even an application. ActiveX controls are commonly found on the Internet and in various applications, including PowerPoint.

If the Trust Center detects a potentially unsafe ActiveX control, it is automatically disabled and you are given the option to enable it.

ActiveX Settings

There are four ActiveX settings to choose from. The three you are most likely to choose are:

- Disable all controls without notification – all controls are disabled and only a red X or a picture of the control will be displayed

- Prompt me before enabling all controls... – this is the default

- Enable all controls without restrictions... – allows any control to run

Changing ActiveX Settings

You can change the setting that the Trust Center uses for ActiveX controls by first accessing the Trust Center.

  Choose ActiveX Settings

Trust Center	? ✕
Trusted Publishers	**ActiveX Settings for all Office Applications**
Trusted Locations	For ActiveX controls in documents not in a trusted location:
Add-ins	○ Disable all controls without notification
ActiveX Settings	○ Prompt me before enabling Unsafe for Initialization controls with additional restrictions and Safe for Initialization (SFI) controls with minimal restrictions
Macro Settings	● Prompt me before enabling all controls with minimal restrictions
Message Bar	○ Enable all controls without restrictions and without prompting (not recommended, potentially dangerous controls can run)
Privacy Options	☑ Safe mode (Helps limit the control's access to your computer)
	OK Cancel

2 Select the setting that you want to use and then click OK

Index